With affection and respect, this book is dedicated to the persons of Hawaii, remarkable individuals every one. Especially do we offer it to the Hawaiians, who continue to show how life can be quickened with joy and graced by laughter.

Contents:

HAWAII'S
enchanted islands

Photography by Ted Czolowski
Text by Jim Sharp

A Q*uest*
Travelbook

RAND McNALLY & COMPANY
Chicago   New York   San Francisco

Introduction

A book of shared pleasures, *Hawaii's enchanted islands* is the personal reaction of two men to what both regard as the most engaging place of life they have experienced.

It is frankly a book celebrating Hawaii's beauty as it appeared—new and fresh—to a highly individual photographer. Equally personal is the choice of selections from Hawaii's history that accompany the photographs. Everything in this book is here solely because it stimulated our interest. We're presenting it because we believe it will interest you.

You'll see unexpected views of the expected tropical beaches of tan sand and coco palms bending in the trade winds. You'll see iron-red earth nurturing crops, economy, and history. Again and again you'll see cold, black volcanic rock: black rock cliffs resisting slashing waves and barren black rock yielding to perky greenery. And you'll see tumbling torrents of the fresh water that makes life possible on these black rocks in the middle of the vast Pacific. Always you'll see the ocean, the endless, impersonal ocean from which these islands arose and into which they will someday return.

You will visit six of the eight major islands, by-passing Niihau and Kahoolawe. Niihau is privately owned and, like private property anywhere (your own living room, for example), is open only to invited guests. Kahoolawe has been eaten bare by goats, bombed bare by the U.S. Navy, and blown bare by the wind; Kahoolawe really doesn't have much to recommend it.

The photographs and text are an effect-and-cause presentation. The photographs show you the beautiful effects of twenty-five million years of natural processes, with a veneer from the two thousand years or so of man's stay here.

Prompted by the photographs, the text chats informally about people and events associated with the subject-matter of each photo. In this relaxed manner, and in more or less chronological order, the carefully researched text provides you with a summary history of Hawaii as you journey from place to place.

During our wandering around the Islands, we plucked no flowers, we gathered no shells, we speared no fish. We did not want to *capture* anything. We wanted merely to enjoy the Islands as they are.

In the same spirit, this book does not seek to capture life in these islands. We sought only to record it as it appeared to us, to record and to share with you some of the wonder and the beauty of Hawaii's enchanted islands.

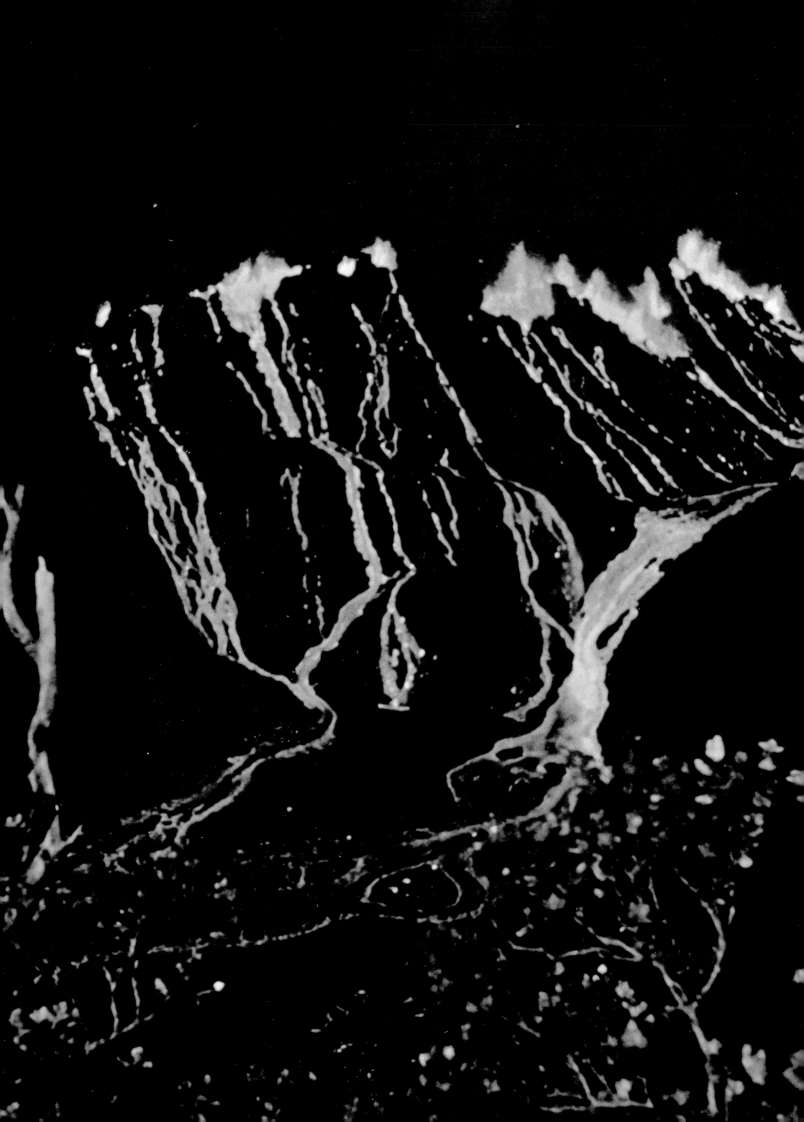

HAWAII

the big island

Twenty-five million years ago the seething innards of this planet broke through its crust. Molten masses boiled up through three miles of ocean depths to form a chain of mountains, some rising two-and-a-half miles above the ocean's surface. This mountain chain lay along an arc across 1600 miles of the North Pacific Ocean.

Cooling rain soaked into the porous rock or trickled down the dome-shaped slopes, etching grooves that were worn into valleys. Incessant seas hammered off huge chunks, leaving abrupt cliffs. Lava continued to pour out from the earth's core, adding more rock until the earth's crust bowed under the weight and the mountains sank. Heat and gas pressure from below pushed them back up. Arctic glaciers melted, adding water to the oceans of the world and flooding islands. Later ice ages drew the water north again, leaving behind marine life on valley floors and coral around island edges. Rain and sun changed black rock to red soil, rich enough to nurture seeds blown or floated in from older, distant lands.

While Greek and Roman galleys were hugging Mediterranean shores, courageous men in double canoes were venturing across 2000-mile stretches of the Pacific Ocean. Some of them came north to the mountain peaks, where they evolved an elaborate civilization, well-suited to these islands. Perhaps in memory of their legendary homeland, Havaiki, they called this land Hawai'i.

Today, *Hawaii* usually means only the eight major islands. Oldest in the north, they are youngest in the south where the Island of Hawaii is still growing through volcanic eruptions. It is here that our trip begins, with a look at how these islands came to be.

Kilauea Caldera is about 400 feet deep.
Across the rim, and to the left, is the Observatory.
To the right, in the background, is Mauna Loa.

Volcanoes tend to be a matter of "either ... or". They are either dome-shaped or cone-shaped. The material that makes them is composed of either gas or liquid. The liquid part is called either magma (while underground as molten rock at a temperature of 2000°F) or lava (after it hits the outside air and "freezes" into rock material). Lava is either *pahoehoe*, a comparatively smooth mass that moves something like a mud slick and looks like molten gold on fire, or *aa*, a cindery, rubbley mass that tumbles and splatters along.

Magma comes from about 35 miles below the earth's surface. If there is a high percentage of gas with the magma, the entire mass explodes straight up. The explosion disintegrates the liquid magma into particles that "freeze" into dust, ash, cinders or bombs. When they fall to earth, their angular edges lock the particles together to form a hard rock called "tuff". Tuff piles up around the earth's vent into a cone with sides as steep as 35° from the horizontal. Examples of such cones are Diamond Head and Punchbowl.

If there is comparatively little gas with the magma, it oozes out of the earth's vent and flows away in the easiest direction. These flows pile into layers that are thinnest at their extremities and thickest around the vent. This builds a dome whose sides slope 3° to 10° from the horizontal. Such were the mountains whose tops are now the islands of Hawaii.

Cold *pahoehoe* flows are shown on page 11. *The cinder cone* (opposite), on the south coast of Puna, is a combination form. It was made when lava flows from Kilauea volcano reached the ocean and exploded. The fragmented lava fell to earth to form a littoral cone, one that is "rootless", or not around a vent.

Hawaii, the biggest of the islands (over twice the size of the seven other major islands combined), was built by five volcanoes. In the south, Mauna Loa and its vent, Kilauea, are still very much alive. Near the Kona Coast, Hualalai was last heard from in 1801. At 13,796 feet, the highest mountain in the chain, Mauna Kea has not erupted since the arrival of men. Northernmost and oldest is Kohala, whose northeastern slopes are the most eroded area on this island.

Volcanoes built these islands; erosion made them habitable. The elements carved sheltered valleys and decomposed black rock into red soil, fertile enough to support a variety of plant life. This, in turn, helped to hold a watershed for a year-round reservoir of fresh water. These high islands provided a variety of altitude, climate, and resources that made an environment where it was possible to establish a society, develop a civilization and create a culture. This the Hawaiians did.

The basic land division in Hawaii was the *ahupuaa*, a wedge or strip of land that ran from the top of a mountain to the sea. Residents of each *ahupuaa* had the full range of resources needed for life in Hawaii.

For household utensils they had bowls and platters carved from hardwood, gourds, and ladles and cups were made from coconut shells. Their tools were adzes, hammers, and chisels of hard basalt, scrapers and awls of shell, files of sharp coral, and needles of bone. Their fishhooks were made of shell or bone.

Their clothing was made of *kapa*, made by soaking and beating the inner bark of the mulberry tree into a paper-like cloth which was then decorated with printed patterns. Women wore only a knee-length skirt, men wore a loincloth called a *malo*.

Communities usually were located near fishing grounds or farming areas. Family dwellings were several thatched huts, each for a different purpose, just as we have separate rooms in our homes.

They lacked beasts of burden, the wheel, and metals. Their culture is known as "stone age", a name that can give the wrong impression. Hawaii was a feudal society, rather like the countries of medieval Europe.

It was divided into three main groups. On the bottom were the *kauwa*, the slaves. In the middle was the largest group, the *makaaina*, the people who lived on the land. They were the farmers, fishermen, laborers, and—when required—the rank and file warriors. At the top were the *alii*, the high-born, noble families. From this group came the chiefs and the priests, as well as most of the administrators, scholars, and artists.

The land was governed by the *kapu*, which still means "forbidden" and, in those days, also meant "sacred". Some traditional *kapu* maintained the divine authority of the gods by forms of worship and rules for daily conduct. These applied to everyone, including the *alii*. Other traditional *kapu* prescribed the degree of veneration to be shown to the highest *alii*, who were believed to be descended from the gods. There were also temporary *kapu* placed on persons, places, or activities by the priests or chiefs.

With the *kapu* system governing it, much of the religion and society of Hawaii was derived from the Kumulipo, the creation chant. Like some books of the Old Testament, it was an attempt by thoughtful men in a pre-scientific society to explain the mysteries of the origin of the world about them and the forces beyond it.

From the Kumulipo came the four main gods worshipped by the Hawaiians: Kane, the god of light and water and life, the creator of man; Ku, the god of war, to whom human sacrifices were made; Kaneloa, the king of the land of the dead; and Lono, the god of agriculture, sports, and peace.

Community services were held at outdoor *heiau*, or temples. Each *heiau* was dedicated to the worship of one god only. The hereditary priests of Ku and Lono were the most important. The priests of Lono were in charge of the Makahiki.

The Makahiki Festival was a period of about four months, from what is now October to February, during the rainy season. It was something like our harvest and thanksgiving. War was *kapu*. Crops were harvested. Taxes were paid. People were freed from their regular labors to enjoy sports, games, and feasting.

After the taxes had been collected, the symbol of Lono, a tall pole with a cross-bar from which hung two wide strips of white *kapa*, appeared to preside over the games.

Upon his return from opening the *Makahiki* around the island, the *alii nui*, or great king of the entire island, had to defend himself against an attack of thrown spears to prove his fighting skill, and thus increase his *mana*, or divine power.

The major source of his *mana* was his genealogical chart, tracing his descent from the gods. This was entrusted to the memory of the court historian.

He was one of the men who had trained their memories to preserve the history and literature of their race by passing it on orally from one generation to the next. For although the Hawaiians had a considerable body of oral literature, they had no written language.

Each of the four major islands (Kauai, Ohau,

Maui, and Hawaii) was ruled by an *alii nui*, who divided his island into *ahupuaa*, each of which was assigned to a favoured *alii*. This chief in turn assigned sections of his district to his followers.

Next to the *alii nui*, the most important man in the kingdom was the *kalaimoku*, a trusted counselor whose role was pretty much that of a prime minister. Directly under him was the *konohiki*, a general executive responsible for seeing that orders were carried out and results achieved.

There was also a group of *kahuna*, most of whom were usually *alii*. Most important of the *kahuna* were the *kahunapule*, or priests, whose role has already been mentioned. *Kahuna* by itself means "expert practitioner" and applied to a fairly large group of masters of skills and knowledge who supervised the major activities needed to preserve and continue the life of the society.

Although this was a highly developed society, well-suited to its environment, much of it could be crippled in a twinkling, for rule in Hawaii was not hereditary. When an *alii nui* died, his title, power, and lands were up for grabs. The prize went to the ablest contending *alii*, who might not even belong to his predecessor's family.

In brief outline, this was the way Hawaii had been living for centuries when, on November 29, 1778, on board a ship off the east coast of Maui, James Cook, a captain in the British Navy, met Kamehameha, a nephew of Kalaniopuu, the *alii nui* of the Island of Hawaii. Although neither of them intended to, between them they were to change the life of old Hawaii forever.

The history of modern Hawaii begins with the birth of Kamehameha on a stormy winter night (probably in 1758) in the northern Kohala district of the island of Hawaii. His parents were of high birth and he was raised and trained as an *alii*.

After the death of his uncle, Kalaniopuu, in 1782, the land was redivided. Kamehameha and five other *alii* of Kohala decided that they had been unfairly treated and went to war. When it was over, Kamehameha was in control of the Kohala, Kona, and Hamakua districts, which comprised the northwestern half of the island.

The next eighteen years were filled with incessant civil war. By 1795 Kamehameha had invaded and conquered all the major islands in the group except Niihau and Kauai. Although he assembled two war fleets for the purpose, he never conquered them, a point of pride among their residents to this day. However, in 1810 the *alii nui* of these islands placed them under the rule of Kamehameha.

Kamehameha had persisted and, in the end, he won. He did what no other man before him had been able to do: he brought all the islands under one rule. He assigned able men to govern each island. He had the land effectively policed and fairly taxed, so that the people could not be exploited by either brigands or government. In his dealings with foreigners, he was both shrewd and scrupulously honest. He made laws which, for the first time in Hawaii, acknowledged that the common man had some rights. But Hawaii remained a feudal society worshipping the old gods.

As late as 1817, several persons were sacrificed for having violated *kapus*. Yet when he lay dying and the priests insisted on sacrifices for him, Kamehameha forbade it, saying: "The men are *kapu* for the king," meaning his son, who was to succeed him. On May 8, 1819, in a grass house a few feet from the ocean that had carried his ancestors and fed his people, Kamehameha . . . "the lonely, lonely one" . . . died.

He was succeeded by his son, Lilolilo, who as Kamehameha II, had a brief reign (1819-1824), notable for one event: the breaking of the *kapu*.

During thirty years of increasing contact with foreigners, many of the *kapu* applying to the *alii* fell by the wayside. Even some of the *kapu* of the gods began to be violated in private. One of these was the eating *kapu*, a *kapu* of the gods that applied to everyone and was particularly harsh on women.

Women could not eat pork, bananas, coconuts, and certain kinds of fish. Women could not eat with men. This *kapu* particularly rankled the high-born women. After the death of Kamehameha, two of his widows, Kaahumanu and the highest-born Keopulani, mother of the young king, got together and applied steady pressure on Lilolilo to break the *kapu* openly.

Although he was probably aware that it was being violated privately, he was understandably reluctant to violate it openly. The king was being urged to destroy a faith, not merely to indulge in eccentric dining habits.

Then, during the first week of November, 1819,

at a feast in Kailua, Kona, the young king sat down and ate with the women. Some of the women then ate foods previously *kapu* to them. At the end of the meal, the king ordered the idols smashed and the temples pulled down.

In one evening he destroyed a religion that went back beyond the horizons of time and had been the central strength of an entire society. When it disappeared, it left a fragmented society and an emotional vacuum.

Into this vacuum and Kailua Bay sailed the brig *Thaddeus* on April 4, 1820. On board was the first company of Protestant missionaries from Boston. The company comprised two ordained ministers, several men trained in useful professions or trades, the wives of all of them, and the children of one couple. The composition of the group helps to explain the success of the American mission in Hawaii. Although the missionaries had no way of knowing it, throughout Polynesia the presence of women in a landing party was always a sign of friendly intentions. The children were a stroke of luck, opening wide the hearts of the child-loving Hawaiians. And, while the ministers might pray fervently for God's help, through the years it was the doctors and artisans (and many of the wives) who lent God a helping hand in ways that helped to convert the Hawaiians.

At first there was some spirited wrangling centering around the young king's reluctance to put on a new moral straight-jacket so soon after having shed the old one. In a few days though, the missionary company was allowed to land and set up shop.

Their greatest lure was writing. The *alii* were fascinated and insisted on being taught. The missionaries put themselves through a crash course in advanced Hawaiian. With the unexpected help of an English missionary with two years experience in Tahiti, they squeezed the melodious Hawaiian language into an alphabet of seven consonants and five vowels, pronounced as they are in French. They printed simple textbooks that were the first appearance of Hawaiian as a written language. Throughout their early years in Hawaii, they were allowed to operate on the condition that first they teach, then preach. By the middle 1830's the Hawaiian Islands probably had a higher literacy rate than that of the United States or Europe of the same time.

Visitors to Hawaii hear so many slogans about the missionaries, that perhaps it is only fair to mention a few details.

Before the Hawaiian field was made independent, Boston sent parties totalling 61 men and 67 women. Most of the missionaries died as they had lived, poor. There were some notable exceptions. For example, the Reverend Amos Cooke became the Cooke of what is now Castle and Cooke.

Before the Second World War many Island businesses were dominated by missionary names; they were there through the efforts of children and grandchildren of the original missionaries. Of hardworking New England stock, these young men were no better or worse than any other businessmen on the make.

The missionaries have been accused of land-grabbing. Before 1848 there was no land to grab; it all belonged to the king and the *alii*. Foreigners lived on it or worked it only by permission, which could be withdrawn any time the owners felt like it. After 1848 the record is not pretty, for reasons that will be gone into later.

It was their attitude toward the Hawaiians that caused the missionaries' downfall, not into lust, but into pride. Most of the evidence comes from the men themselves in their writings. A reader can get the strong impression that the missionaries simply could not accept the Hawaiians as equals before God. A questionable attitude in any man, it was fatal in a missionary. The missionaries labored hard on behalf of the Hawaiians, but in time their sin of pride was to turn many of the Hawaiians against them.

For in the beginning, faced with the choice that every Polynesian island had to make between traders and merchants on one side, and missionaries on the other, the Hawaiian *alii* came down firmly on the side of the missionaries—and saw to it that their people did too. On their part, the missionaries educated the Hawaiians in western ways; did their best to prevent them from being cheated by traders; did what they could to slow down the rapid decline of the Hawaiian population from germs usually brought by trading ships; and recruited the best men they could find to help the Hawaiians administer an increasingly complex government. Away from Honolulu, many of the missionaries did come to love their parishioners and were loved in return. It is sad that for all their labours on behalf of the Hawaiians, in which they spared themselves least of all, a handful of them should have left a legacy of bitterness and contempt.

Orchids (far right) grow well in volcanic cinders because they hold moisture, yet provide good drainage. The field on page 17 is in the Puna district. With the Hilo district north of it, Puna grows many of the tons of flowers that make Hawaii the "Orchid Island," and the city of Hilo the orchid capital of the world.

Skeletons of 'ohi'a trees along the half-mile Devastation Trail in Volcano National Park.

19

Along the Kona Coast is the *City of Refuge* National Park at Honaunau. If they could outrun their pursuers, defeated warriors, noncombatants, and *kapu* breakers would be safe from any authority once they were inside the walls (left edge of picture) of the *pu'uhonua*, or place of refuge.

Two Mauna Keas:
the mountain rising ou
of the picture to the lef
the beach resort on
Kawaiahae Bay in the
foreground.

Kailua Bay and tow
The crescent-shap
hotel to the left of
pier is on the site
Kamehameh
residen

St. Benedict's Catholic Church near Keokea
The naturalistic murals were done with housepaint
by a Belgian priest in 1912.

Weighing a marlin from the waters off Kailua-Kona,
where the deep-sea fishing draws sportsmen
from all over the world.

Surf-casters at Kalapapa Park and a pair of idlers a few miles to the east on the south coast of Puna. Both locations are *black sand beaches*. They were made by lava hissing into the sea and exploding into beads and threads of black glass, which were then ground down by the action of the waves. These beaches have a porous surface that tends to tame roaring surf to a fizzing froth.

On the Waimea Plateau, 4,000 feet above sea level, are some of the 40,000 head or so of Hereford cattle that roam the quarter million acres of the *Parker Ranch*, the largest ranch in the United States under single ownership.

Kona coffee

'Ohi'a Lehua

Anthuriums

"a discovery which, though the last, seemed in many respects to be the most important . . . made by Europeans throughout the Pacific Ocean" was the estimate of the Hawaiian Islands by Captain James Cook in the journal of his third voyage.

Cook's two ships, the *Resolution* and the *Discovery* had left Bora Bora and were sailing north in search of a water passage through North America. At dawn of January 18, 1778 they sighted Oahu, then Kauai. They landed at Kauai, where they spent two weeks before continuing north.

After leaving Kauai, Cook surveyed the American coast northward from Latitude 45° N., much of the coasts of Alaska and Siberia, and entered the Arctic. He concluded that there was no water

passage across North America. With winter coming on, Cook headed south toward Hawaii, which he had named the Sandwich Islands. During the eight months Cook had been away, the story of his arrival spread through the islands. Hawaiians remembered that Lono had left the Islands in an odd-shaped canoe, promising to return someday during the *Makahiki*. The sails hanging from the spars of Cook's square-rigged ships may have suggested the festival banner of Lono when the ships appeared off the north coast of Maui on November 26, 1778, during the *Makahiki* season. They were visited by the *alii nui* of Maui. Four days later, off the east coast of Maui, the ships were greeted by the *alii nui* of Hawaii with a retinue of chiefs, including the young Kamehameha. After this, Cook sailed south around Hawaii and up the west coast to Kealakekua Bay where, on January 17, 1779, he dropped anchor.

Their reception was lively. Hawaiians swarmed out to his ships. Cook estimated that there were as many as a thousand canoes in the bay. They came out on surfboards. They swam out in shoals.

The officers went ashore on the north side of the bay to pay their respects to the *alii nui* of Hawaii, Kalaniopuu. Later, they were taken to the south shore of the bay, to Hikau Heiau, where Cook was honored with religious services and a feast.

"The meaning of the various ceremonies with which we had been received . . . can only be the subject of conjectures," wrote Lieutenant King, who completed Cook's journal of his third voyage. "They were . . . without doubt, expressive of high respect . . . and, as related to the person of Captain Cook, they seemed approaching to adoration."

Relations were cordial during their stay. Cook wrote of the Hawaiians: "They are an open, candid, active people . . . no people could trade with more honesty than these." The Hawaiians were generous with their provisions. Knowing how useful it was, the Englishmen gave them as much metal as they could safely spare. Cook had the party's armorer forge iron daggers patterned after the Hawaiian *pahoa*, a two-foot-long dagger, pointed at both ends.

While the crews improved their health after the long Arctic voyage, Cook learned as much as he could of this new society. Cook started his first voyage as a naval officer with a high reputation as a navigator and cartographer. The experiences of his three voyages had enlarged his scientific interests. He had become a very good naturalist and anthropologist. He was interested in everything.

In his dealings with the many new people to whom he brought the doubtful advantages of civilization, he was always considerate. His attitude towards their societies and beliefs was free from condescension. He was interested in them and he took them pretty much as he found them. Though not in the manor born, this captain who rose from the ranks was a gentleman in spirit and in conduct.

As such, he couldn't help but notice that it was time to go. It was the middle of the rainy season, Kona was not a richly fertile area, and the abundant *Makahiki* harvest had long been used. With the well-being of his own people in mind, Kalaniopuu began making discreet inquiries about a sailing date. Cook told him. On the evening of their sailing, the ships were all but swamped with farewell gifts of vegetables, hogs, and *kapa* cloth (whose patterns Cook considered the most beautiful he had seen). Among items given in return by the English was a complete tool chest. On February 4, 1779, the ships sailed north.

On February 7th a gale sprung the foremast of the *Resolution*. Both vessels returned to Kealakekua Bay, where Cook knew they had eaten away their welcome. Although slightly strained, relations continued to be friendly, and the crews took the broken mast ashore to repair it.

On the morning of the 14th, a cutter was missing from the *Discovery*. Cook decided to bring the king on board and hold him as a hostage until the missing article was returned.

He posted a cordon of boats across the entrance to the bay to stop any canoe attempting to leave.

He armed himself with a double-barreled musket, loading one barrel with bird shot, the other barrel with deadly ball. Then, between seven and eight in the morning, he got into a six-oared pinnace with Lieutenant Molesworth Phillips and nine marines. From the north end of the bay, he ordered Lieutenant John Williamson to bring his launch and stand by in case of trouble. Why was Cook acting so rashly and brutally toward people he liked and respected?

His three expeditions had taken him along the malaria-ridden shores of Melanesia, into the ice-flows of Antarctica, through the reef-infested waters off Australia, and north into the Arctic Ocean. By this fateful morning, those voyages had covered a period a few days shy of ten-and-a-half years; eight-and-a-half of those years Cook had spent at sea in ships a little over a hundred feet in length. Even for the captain, an eighteenth century sailing ship was not a Matson cruise. The broken mast was the last of a long series of troubles that had plagued his third voyage owing to disgraceful outfitting by corrupt suppliers. Captain James Cook was tired and he was fifty years old.

Cook, Phillips, and the nine marines landed on the slippery black rocks along the shore. After ordering the boats to stand by clear of the rocks, Cook and his men marched to Kalaniopuu's residence.

Kalaniopuu had just awakened and came out to greet the party in a friendly manner. After a short conversation, Cook was convinced that Kalaniopuu knew nothing about the stolen cutter. Cook invited him to spend the day on the *Resolution*, which Kalaniopuu readily consented to do, and the party started walking toward the boats.

Before they could reach the shore, the queen and several *alii* rushed to them and pleaded with Kalaniopuu not to go. Two of the *alii* respectfully, but firmly, forced Kalaniopuu to sit down.

Hawaiians began gathering around them. At this time of year, with war forbidden, many of Kalaniopuu's experienced warriors were near their aged *alii nui*. The foreigners' ways were new to them, but to a Polynesian an armed landing party that stayed in formation, with manned boats waiting close to shore, meant just one thing. They thronged more closely around Cook and Kalaniopuu.

The crowd hemmed in the marines so tightly that they could not use their muskets if they had to. Lt. Phillips moved his men out of the crowd, and drew them up along the rocks close to the water's edge.

Puzzled muttering was turning into a base rumble. Cook could hear the excited shouts of more people hurrying to the scene. Possibly alarmed by the sound of firing from across the bay, many of the new arrivals were carrying spears, clubs, *pahoas*, and stones.

Cook abandoned his plan and started toward the shore. Just then news arrived that the foreigners had fired on a canoe, killing a high-ranking *alii*. Women and children disappeared. Armed warriors began tying on their armor of matting.

One of them advanced on Cook, threatening him with an iron *pahoa*. Cook fired his barrel of bird-shot, which bounced harmlessly off the chest mat. The warriors became bolder. One moved to stab the captain. Cook fired his other barrel, loaded with ball, killing the man. Cook and the marines became targets for a flurry of stones.

The marines on shore and the men in the boats opened fire without waiting for orders from Captain Cook. The angry, shouting Hawaiians moved toward the shore.

Cook turned, either to order the men to cease fire or to call the boats in. He was pelted with rocks. The Hawaiians were almost on top of him.

They had already reached the marines along the shore. Before they could re-load their muzzle-loading muskets, the marines were overwhelmed. Four of them were caught among the slippery rocks and killed. Of the five marines remaining, three were dangerously wounded. Lt. Phillips was stabbed in the back by an iron *pahoa*. Having held his fire, he shot his attacker. Phillips ordered his men to the boats.

Some of the men in the boats tried to keep up a steady fire in the midst of others who stayed at their oars, trying to control the pitching and rolling of the small crafts in the turbulent surf. During all this time, both boats were not farther than twenty yards from the shore. In the launch, Lt. Williamson watched, while precious seconds sped by.

As he neared the water's edge, Cook was struck on the back by a club. He dropped his musket and staggered a few steps more. He called again to the boats. As Cook reached the water's edge, he was stabbed in the back with an iron *pahoa*. He fell face forward into knee-deep water. He managed to raise his head and look towards the boats, which still did not come in.

The marines were stumbling, wading, and swimming towards the pinnace. Lieutenant Phillips was the last man aboard. The launch under Williamson had already left for the safety of the ships.

Captain Cook was last seen alive clinging to a rock, before being enveloped by warriors.

The beach was packed solid with Hawaiians. The ships' cannons opened fire, burrowing ugly holes in the living mass. The crowd scattered. The black beach was deserted, except for the mangled remains of Captain James Cook, four Hawaiian *alii*, four English marines, and twenty-five Hawaiian commoners.

On this beach today a plaque and a monument honor Captain Cook. There is nothing commemorating the Hawaiians "though they, too," as Stanley Porteus pointed out, "died for king and country".

Tempers stayed high while leaders on both sides did their best to control their own groups and resume friendly relations. Anxious as both sides were for the ships to sail, the English would not leave until the body of Captain Cook was returned. After considerable negotiation, they received a bundle containing most of the bones and pieces of flesh.

The Hawaiians had taken the body and stripped the flesh from it so that the bones could be distributed among the *alii*, according to rank. It was considered that the bones of an *alii* possessed *mana*, or divine power. Although they had killed him in anger, the Hawaiians regarded Captain Cook as a great chief.

They did not eat the flesh. The Hawaiians were not cannibals. Even the most energetic research by their detractors has been unable to produce any reliable proof that they were cannibals.

On the evening of February 22, 1779, the two ships sailed north for further surveying. The day before they left, they held services committing Cook's soul to God, then lowered his remains into the bay the Hawaiians called Kealakekua.

There is an irony in this that goes beyond mere human accident. Whether as the pagan god Lono, returning in human form, or a Christian whose soul was setting out on its last great journey, James Cook could not have chosen a more appropriate place. Translated literally, Kealakekua means "pathway of the gods".

Lumbering along with the trade winds, saturated clouds hit the northeastern slopes of Mauna Kea and are squeezed into uncounted numbers of streams. Older streams have often cut their valleys back to abrupt drops, such as that made when Kolekole Stream dives 420 feet as *Akaka Falls* (left), celebrated in a haunting song.

Following the path of least resistance, these streams gallivant downhill until they plunge from cliffs into the sea along the *Hamakua Coast* (right), the fertile fringe of Mauna Kea from Waipio Valley to Hilo. Long the domain of "King" Cane (bottom, right), this area is being flecked with groves of Macadamia trees (center, right) whose hard-shelled, crunchy nut is becoming a great favorite in gourmet shops across the mainland. Shaded by ferns or tangerine trees, row after row of *anthuriums* (bottom) grow in the black ash of Puna around the village of Pahoa.

Across the island, on 5,000 acres of rich soil terraced across slopes 800 to 2,000 feet above the sea, grows *Kona Coffee* (page 25 bottom). Morning sun, afternoon shade, and occasional evening showers provide the ideal climate that has helped make Kona (as one expert described it) "one of the world's four great coffees". Farther up the west coast is *Kohala*, where you'll find the settlement shown on the next page.

Kohala (coast)

Hawaii's northeast coast (left) shows how wind-driven water has eroded deep valleys and slashed steep cliffs into a massive dome of barren rock. The same thing happened to the windward sides of all the islands, although they may not look the same because of their different ages.

Water evaporating from waves was gathered up and rolled into clouds by trade winds running toward the islands from the northeast. When these clouds hit the mass of mountain they were deflected upward, where cooler air condensed them into rain. This was absorbed by the porous rock of the young volcanoes. Over millions of years, these falling drops alternated with the hot sun to change particles of rock into soil. This soil sealed the lava's pores and the water rolled downhill, along the path of least resistance.

Grains of soil and ash, picked up or torn off along the way, acted as tools, grinding the stream bed deeper. As banks were exposed to the air, they decomposed and collapsed, widening the valley. A dominant stream would "capture" the other streams in its area, and the increased volume of water would cut deeper and wider.

While this was going on, the same winds had been slamming tons of sea against the shore, tearing off huge rocks. These were thrown back against the cliffs. Heavy, steady hammering by waves cut a horizontal trough into the side of the cliffs, a few feet above and a few feet below sea level.

When this undercutting became severe enough, the rock above it collapsed into the sea. Instead of splintering or sloping, the resulting cliffs stand clean and vertical, largely due to the structure of basalt, the major rock form created by the lavas of Hawaii.

Connoisseurs of these Islands often pick the Big Island of Hawaii as their favorite because it has everything the others have—plus volcanoes. Volcanoes are certainly distinctive. Their behavior is lively, their effects fascinating. Perhaps we have shown you too much of them and, in so doing, have been unfair to Hawaii's abundance of natural beauty in more conventional forms.

A few miles before Mauna Kea slopes into Hilo Bay, the Wailuku River cascades over *Rainbow Falls* (right). Even volcanoes have their softer aspects: high on the slopes of Kilauea is the *Tree Fern Forest* (left), a lush, green prelude to our next island.

KAUAI *the garden island*

The oldest and most eroded, storm-battered, and rain-soaked of the group, Kauai is where visitors and movie-makers discover the sunny, South Sea island of their dreams.

Kauai is an island of contrasts and contradictions.

Kauai is a single mountain mass with a crescent of fertile land around its eastern and southern shores. The mountain is named Waialeale, although its highest point at 5,243 feet, is named Kawaikini.

Whether or not it's *the* wettest spot on earth, Mt. Waialeale manages to maintain an annual rainfall of about 460 inches, with one year reported at 624. Stretches of land at Waialeale's western perimeter are almost desert.

Mt. Waialeale isn't even a volcanic mountain; it's the contents of a volcano. The caldera of the volcano that formed much of Kauai was possibly the largest in the Islands. Inside the caldera were layer upon layer of ponded lava, which, because it was confined, cooled slowly and pressed down on previous layers. This created a much tougher lava than is usual. Much of the original volcano has disappeared; Waialeale is the heavily eroded remains of its tougher contents.

The north shore coves between Haena and Hanalei have been the backgrounds for many movies that wanted to show a tropical island at its sunny best.

A few miles to the east, a gauge on Kilauea Plantation recorded 40 inches of rain during the 24 hours following the evening of January 24, 1956; of this, six inches fell in a single half-hour. The scientist who reported this suggested it may have been close to being the heaviest known world rainfall.

When they gave the island its original name of *Kauai-a-mamo-ka-lani-pono*, "the-fountainhead-of-many-waters-from-on-high-and-bubbling-up-from-below", the always poetic ancient Hawaiians were stunned into a mere factual statement.

Any ordinary island would be satisfied with the factual distinctions Kauai possesses, but Kauai is no ordinary island. Kauai has legends the way some places in the Islands have mynah birds: you can't escape them.

One group of legends fascinates scholars. These concern the *menehune*.

The *menehune* were a legendary race of energetic sprites about two feet tall who worked only at night, completed every project in one night or not at all, and were paid with shrimp. They are credited with building the wall of Alakeko Fishpond and digging an irrigation ditch above Waimea, on the South Shore. While these may not have been built by flying squads of nocturnal midgets, *somebody* built them.

From the scant evidence available these islands probably had been the home of people originally from the Marquesas. Due to an inferior culture and a limited diet, they were probably smaller than the Tahitians who invaded and conquered these islands from the 11th to 14th centuries. The Tahitians then settled down for four centuries of good living.

In January of 1778, Captain James Cook first set foot on Hawaiian soil at Kauai's Waimea, starting Hawaii's visitor industry.

A few years after Cook's arrival, Kamehameha began the conquest that brought under his control all the islands except Kauai and Niihau, a point of pride among residents of these islands to this day. In 1810 Kauai was placed, voluntarily, under Kamehameha's authority by its *alii nui*, Kaumualii.

His son, George P. Kaumualii, was probably the first Hawaiian to be wounded in action while serving with the United States armed forces; he was in the American Navy during the War of 1812.

In later years Kauai could claim the first commercially successful sugar plantation, the first sugar mill, and the first coffee grown in commercially successful quantities in Hawaii.

But in calling itself the Garden Island, Kauai makes the best claim of all. It does rain heavily in spots but the rich land blooms colorfully all year, like the African Tulip Tree (left), whose cluster of red flowers blossom a few at a time so that the tree is in full color the year round.

Perhaps 5,000 years ago Caucasians left the valleys of India for southeast Asia, where they met and mingled with Monguls from the north. These people moved down Malaysia and across Indonesia until, about 4,000 years ago, they were on the eastern shores of Indonesia, watching the sun rise above the empty Pacific.

They had the courage—and the skill—to sail out across this unknown ocean until they could find their way through the sparse islands of Micronesia to the Gilbert Islands. From here, some may have continued east to Hawaii. Most of them apparently sailed south to Samoa and Tonga. They may have been joined by others from Indonesia who had worked their way along the coasts of the high, dark islands of Melanesia.

After the limited resources of the small, low islands of Micronesia, the lush, high islands of the Samoan group provided these voyagers with an environment in which they could stay long enough to become recognizably what we know today as Polynesian in their appearance, their culture, and their knowledge of the sea. The similarity of those people on widely separated islands suggests that new islands were settled by colonizing expeditions containing a representative cross-section of the society at home so that the settlers could establish a community similar to the one they had left.

From sixty to over a hundred feet in length, the Polynesian voyaging canoe was two deep canoes with a platform across them large enough to accommodate up to a hundred people for the three to four weeks their provisions would last. Under average conditions the ship could make about five to seven knots, for an average day's run of about 120 miles. With favorable winds, this could be bettered. When the wind died, the men could paddle in round-the-clock relays.

The Polynesians were probably more at home on the sea than any other race of men in history. They navigated using the stars (they knew and could name about 150), deep swells, waves, wind direction, the position of the sun and its shadow, and the flights of birds.

After centuries in Samoa the increasing population outgrew the food supply, producing two inevitable actions: war and emigration. Polynesians sailed into the sunrise again, through the Cook Islands to Tahiti, which in time developed into the center of Eastern Polynesia.

Recent excavations on the Island of Hawaii suggest that somebody from the Marquesas Islands was here around 194 A.D., perhaps even earlier. They lived in these islands for centuries, yet we know little about them. They left behind some tantalizing mysteries, including the *Alakeko Fishpond* (right), south of Lihue.

Whoever they were, they were here when the Tahitians arrived during the 11th century. This was the beginning of three centuries of voyaging throughout Polynesia that may have been due to religious wars or over-population in Tahiti. Whatever the cause, it resulted in the settlement of New Zealand and the conquest of these islands.

The Tahitians brought many new forms of plant and animal life, a new religion, and a higher form of society, which they imposed on the conquered residents. Near the end of the 14th century, the long voyages came to an end. What had become Hawaii settled down for four centuries of splendid isolation until one morning in January, 1778.

The windward east coast of Kauai is rich in soil and history, much of the second is due to the first. The red earth of Kauai nurtured the first successful sugar plantation in the Islands. This in turn gave Kauai the first irrigation ditch for sugar, and the first sugar mill. The old mill was in the same area as the present *sugar mill* (right, center) on the flat plains of Koloa, the southeastern district of Kauai.

North of Koloa, on the other side of Hoary Head Range, is Nawiliwili. It is Kauai's major harbor and the seaport of Lihue, the county seat. Nawiliwili has a massive bulk storage plant from which sugar is loaded into freighters by conveyor belt. This is off to the left of the picture (top, right), which shows the Kauai Surf Resort sunning itself on Nawiliwili's *Kalapaki Beach*.

Farther up the east coast is the old royal area along the Wailua River. Across the road from the Wailua River, beyond bougainvillea and hala (pandanus) trees, is *Opaekaa Falls* (left). Its name means "rolling shrimp" because of the abundance of the tasty rascals once found in the pool below the falls.

A good deal farther north, near Anahola, are fields of pineapple being harvested below the *Hole in the Mountain* (bottom, right). Legend says that this hole was made by a spear thrown by a giant. Two-foot-tall construction workers and belligerent giants: even when forming legends, Kauai is an island of contrasts.

The first Tahitians to reach Kauai landed at the mouth of the Wailua River. It is justly called the royal area. The great chief Puna settled here and his descendants became the "bluebloods" of Hawaiian *alii*. Any child of royal blood had to be born here to be recognized as an *alii* of the highest rank. From about 1830 to 1850, Deborah Kapule, the last queen of Kauai, made her home on the land now occupied by the *Coco Palms Hotel* (bottom, left).

Beyond here, on the other side of the road, is *Holo-Holo-Ku Heiau* (center, left). Generally considered to be Kauai's oldest, it is the first of seven *heiaus* that were located from the mouth of the river to the top of Mt. Waialeale. Joining them was a *kapu* royal road, the lower part of which is a public highway today.

Wailua translates literally as "two waters". The "royal road" runs alongside the northern branch of the river. About halfway up the southern branch is *Wailua Falls* (top, left).

For a leisurely view of the area, you can take one of the sightseeing boats to the *Fern Grotto* (right). Inside the grotto, at times when a Hawaiian couple have joined voices and caressed the air with *Ke Kali Ne Au* (The Hawaiian Wedding Song), strong men have been known to sob aloud.

Hawaii is America's only Polynesian state.

It is the northern apex of a triangle about 4,500 miles on each side from Hawaii to New Zealand to Easter Island and back to Hawaii. Within this triangle is an area of some twelve million square miles of open ocean flecked with islands that have a total land area— omitting New Zealand—less than that of the state of Maryland.

These islands were grouped together under the name Polynesia ("many islands") because of the striking racial and cultural similarities of their residents.

Rarely seen by anyone, the top of Mt. Waialeale (above) is usually shrouded by clouds. The rain gauge at the left records yearly totals that usually run to about 460 inches.

On this summit is a sacred pool (below) to which Hawaiians once made annual pilgrimages to leave offerings.

Bounded by cliffs 2,000 to 3,000 feet high is *Kalalau Valley* (left), one of the hidden valleys of the northwest Na Pali region.

Waimea Canyon is in large part the result of a fault, or fracture, of the earth's surface. This opening caused the thin-bedded, sloping lavas of the original volcano cone to collapse toward it, thus falling away from the heavy, hard-packed layers of lava inside the volcano. You are on the west, or collapsed, side of the canyon, looking across to the east wall. The banded pattern on the opposite wall is made by the horizontal layers of hard lava once inside the volcano basin.

Waimea Canyon's remarkable size owes much to its direction. When the lava cracked, it opened a cut almost at right angles to the pattern of streams running from the mountain top to the sea. The canyon then swallowed the water from all these streams, causing a faster and deeper gouging than would occur during the normal development of a valley by stream erosion. Adding to this, most of the northern streams falling into Waimea Canyon are from Alakai Swamp.

The Alakai Swamp is not really a conventional swamp at all. It is about 20 square miles of rolling hills and heavy vegetation at about 4,000 to 5,000 feet above sea level. It stretches up the northern slopes to the top of Mt. Waialeale and receives its full share of the heavy rainfall. But the rain does not sink into the porous lava rock because the bottom of Alakai Swamp is sealed with colloidal soils of a type not known to exist anywhere else in the Islands. The rain accumulates in a reservoir until its volume begins to drain off at the lowest point. In doing this, it has carved many of the valleys of the Na Pali coast, north of Alakai Swamp, and contributed mightily to the erosion of Waimea Canyon.

Today the canyon is reported to be from 10 to 14½ miles long and from 2,750 to 3,657 feet deep. (After you've been here for a while, you'll find that in Hawaii it's difficult to get people to agree about *anything*.)

Its dimensions are irrelevant; its beauty is unforgettable. The colors of its walls change with the passing minutes, are fleetingly veiled by sudden cloud shadows, and are complemented by the soft green of the trees clustered along its gentler slopes. Lingering visitors gazing down at Waimea Canyon's kaleidoscope have occasionally been startled to see wild goats gazing right back at them.

Snoozing for centuries is the *Sleeping Giant* (top), south of Kapaa. Wide awake, though, on the northernmost point of Kauai, is *Kilauea Lighthouse* (bottom). Its clamshell lens, the largest in the world, is a landfall for ships and planes from the Orient. Naupaka bushes nearby serve as a spring and summer nursery for fuzzy, blue-faced booby birds.

"Movie Island" could be the nickname for Kauai. Much of the beauty of *South Pacific*, for example, came from its scenes filmed around Hanalei Bay (far left). *Bird of Paradise* was another Kauai film, as well as the name of the dashing flower at the right. With so many others doing it, Kauai has little need to blow its own horn, although it does on the south shore, near Poipu. The *Spouting Horn* (center) sounds off with an eerie moan when in-rushing surf is forced up through holes in the rocks to spray into geysers.

The sunset torch-lighting ceremony was started by the Coco Palms Hotel. The Kauai Surf Resort has made it amphibious, an appropriately Polynesian touch. Out of the shadows run young Hawaiians, lighting the laua torches that fringe the beach. From the water's edge come the blasts of conch shells and the boom of a sharkskin *pahu* (drum). Their ceremony over, with their flaming torches held aloft the young men paddle away across the darkening waters.

The red soil of Hawaii is rich in the wrong kind of iron. The iron oxide in the soil is linked with manganese oxide in a form the plants cannot absorb. For years the planters have had to spray the iron-rich soil with an iron solution to help feed their plants.

To make sugar cane easier to harvest and cleaner to process, the fields are set on fire before harvesting. This destroys the dry tangle of useless material and leaves the ripe cane—87 percent liquid—unharmed.

Hanalei Bay with the Plantation Hotel in the left foreground.

53

Hanohano Hanalei ... "glorious Hanalei"
... the song tells us, and rightly so,
whether celebrating the bay, the river, or
its bordering *Hanalei Valley* (top left).

Now checkered with taro and rice
patches, the valley once glistened with
nothing but rice paddies. Silk, cotton,
and the first coffee in commercial
quantities, were grown in Hanalei. From
this valley on the north shore, large
quantities of oranges were shipped to
California, long before that area grew its
own. These grew from seeds left by
Captain George Vancouver. Although
he was later in charge of expeditions that
visited Hawaii, Vancouver first saw these
islands as an officer serving under
Captain Cook.

Cook's ships sighted Kauai on
January 18, 1778. The next day they
found suitable anchorage in *Waimea Bay*,
off the south coast (bottom, left). Cook
stepped ashore somewhere along the
beach to the right. One of his ships was
visited by a young couple introduced as
the king and queen of Kauai. This is
probably true, for, although Wailue was
the sacred royal area, Kauai seems to have
been ruled from Waimea. Here the
rulers could keep an eye on their nearby
possession, the island of Niihau.

Waimea is also the site of the ruins of
a Russian Fort (off to the left of the
picture area). It is all that remains of an
attempt by a German physician to seize
the Islands for the Russian Czar in 1817.
Kamehameha heard of this and ordered
the governor of Kauai to get rid of the
Russians. He did.

One of the hundreds of waterfalls in the
steep, sheltered interior of Kauai.
Previously seen only by guides and
hunters, they can now be visited by
anyone using a helicopter.

Like battle-scarred veterans, the 3,000 foot ramparts of *Na Pali* coast show the signs of their losing fight against the forces of wind and water. Between them they shelter lush valleys that were once the home of hundreds of Hawaiians. Together, they help protect the vast watershed behind them. Within this watershed wilderness grow plants found nowhere else in the Islands—or in the world.

Shelter from the fiercer elements, rich soil, abundant water, and a variety of plant life, with the warm encouragement of the sun, help to produce a garden. Aptly named the Garden Island, Kauai provides abundant means of living and tangible beauty to make that living good. More than that, the quiet hospitality of this island paradise offers peace of heart and mind.

MAUI

the valley island

Maui is an in-between place.

Historically, it is the bridge between the traditions of old Hawaii and the rumbling beginnings of modern Hawaii. Geographically, it is the main island between Oahu and Hawaii. Physically, it is the island formed when the older West Maui Mountains were joined to the slopes of Haleakala by a seven-mile-wide isthmus from which Maui gets its nickname: "the Valley Island".

Being between Hawaii and Oahu, Maui was often invaded by the forces of one on their way to the other. Occasionally Maui's rulers would return the calls, with lively results.

When Kamehameha III moved to Lahaina, Maui, the capital was where the king was. When he moved the capital to Honolulu, he was moving something besides his own person. By then Hawaii was a constitutional monarchy with a legislature, a supreme court, and a body of written laws.

Lahaina, Maui, was host to the whaling fleets that kept the kingdom's economy afloat between the early boom in sandalwood and the later support of sugar.

While whaling was dying out, men were learning how to bring mountain reservoirs to thirsty sugar cane miles away. Soon Maui's sandy central plains turned green with tasseled cane.

On this central plain, or valley, today Maui's business runs between the new port city of Kahului and, three miles inland, the old county seat of Wailuku. On Wailuku's main street is the *Royal Poinciana* (or *Flamboyant* or *Flame*) *Tree*, opposite, with the spire of Kaahumanu Church rising behind it.

The island's tourism stretches between old-style Hana and new-style Kaanapali Beach. Down in the Hawaiian country area of Hana every effort is made to keep the easy charm the way it's been for years. Up at

Kaanapali, developers have taken a beautiful beach and several dozen acres of former cane fields and are demonstrating that a large-scale visitor resort area can be built so as to enhance the beauty of its location for years to come, if it is thoroughly planned and carefully controlled.

For even when participating in Hawaii's statehood economy, this lovely, country island is going about it calmly and intelligently in Maui's own way, at Maui's own pace.

Any mention of Maui might as well start where the action was, on the sunset coast of West Maui, at Lahaina, during the days when whalers were bellowing around the Pacific. A rich, sperm-whale area was discovered off the coast of Japan around 1820, and the whaling fleets—most of them out of New England ports—made for the Pacific. Japan was closed to foreigners. Hawaii lay along their route, a natural place to rest and take on supplies. From 1823 to 1840, about a hundred whaling ships a year put in at Honolulu or Lahaina.

Whaling rarely attracted the daintiest members of a community. When they made port they had been at sea for six months of hard, dangerous, dirty work. Fifty ships with, say 25 to 30 men per ship, meant that Lahaina was about to receive 1,250 to 1,500 men for whom there was "no law west of the horn". To protect the Hawaiians, the missionaries tried to have blue laws passed. Their reasons may have been Biblical, but they were also hygienically sound. Often rulers tried to enforce these laws. When holders of these opposing points of view met, the results were often vivacious.

New whaling grounds in the Pacific were discovered in 1840 and the traffic increased. From 1845 to 1855 the number of ships reached their highest point. The price of whale oil was increasing. There seemed to be no limit. Unknown to these men, this was the beginning of the end. In 1859 petroleum was discovered in Pennsylvania; one of its by-products, kereosene, began replacing whale oil in lamps. From 1860 to 1865 Confederate warships in the Pacific found rich hunting that included many Yankee whalers. In 1872 most of the remaining whaleships were destroyed in an arctic ice floe.

By then, the capital had been in Honolulu for more than two decades. In four years, the Reciprocity Treaty was to make sugar crown prince in a land where it soon replaced the Hawaiian as king. Lahaina settled down to a long—and probably welcome—slumber from which it is now being awakened with restoration programs and new crews of visitors of a more restrained nature than the whalers.

Most visitors to Maui reach Lahaina by road south from Wailuku, past Maalaea, around the point and

north along the west coast. By doing this, they avoid some challenging driving; but they miss exciting scenery and some of the most beautiful beaches in the Islands. Let's take Kahekili Highway along the east coast (opposite) and around the northern curve of Maui.

Cactus and Norfolk pines on Maui's north curve

Near the northern end of Kahekili Highway

Orchids along the highway

Off the northwest coast of Maui lies Kapulua Bay. Curving along its edge is *Kapalua*, or *Fleming's Beach*. Many visitors call this the most beautiful beach in all the islands. Swimming is safe here and the shady park has picnic tables and rest rooms.

Golf course at the Kaanapali Beach Resort, Kekaa, or Black Rock, in the background.

Torch Ginger.

Looking south to Lahaina with Lanai in the distance

Oleander beside a cane field

Lahaina waterfront, the Courthouse (1859) in the center.

Above Lahaina is Lahainaluna School, a secondary school started in 1831. On its campus is *Hale Pa'i* (below), built in 1836 to house the press used to print the newspaper, *Ka Lama Hawaii*, two years earlier. The school and the newspaper were the first ones, not only in Hawaii, but west of the Rockies. Below it is a reconstructed corner of the *old fort* on the waterfront. From 1832 to 1854 it served as a city jail.

Pioneer Inn, renovated and enlarged.

Early morning quiet south of town.

Maximum rainfall in Hawaii usually occurs between altitudes of 2,000 and 6,000 feet. Puu Kukui, the highest point of the West Maui Mountains is 5,788 feet above sea level. These *rain clouds* (left) have managed to just squeeze over the windward side to drench cane fields on the western slopes.

Rising 1,200 feet from the valley floor, Iao Needle is an isolated remnant of the giant caldera of the ancient West Maui Mountain.

The needle looks as lonely as a sentinel standing guard over this sad valley of bloodshed. For it was into Iao Valley that Kamehameha's invading army pushed the defending forces under Kalanikupule in 1790. The resulting battle produced a slaughter that was said to have caused the stream to run red for three days and three nights from the corpses that dammed it.

Within the spectacular beauty of the picture at the far right is the laboratory where sugar was transformed from an irritating possibility to an irrigated fortune.

Sugar cane had grown here before Cook arrived. The Hawaiians used it for hedges. Early foreigners made several attempts to grow it for commercial use. None were successful. Even the first large plantation at Koloa, Kauai, took 13 years to get on its feet. With perfect weather and rich soil, the missing ingredient was a reliable supply of enough water. To produce a pound of sugar requires a ton of water.

In 1856 the Lihue Plantation irrigation ditch on Kauai proved that water can be carried for miles to provide an abundant and controlled supply for thirsty cane fields. Below the crest in the foreground of the picture are the slopes where two missionaries' sons, Alexander and Baldwin, tapped the reservoirs inside Haleakala. By the time they were through, their Hamakua Ditch had cost $80,000 and ran 17 miles, but it had a capacity of forty million gallons of fresh water a day. Sugar was on its way.

The fertile plain below you in the photo contains the largest sugar plantation in the world.

The back-breaking labor that required the tens of thousands of immigrants who came to Hawaii during the past century, is now done largely by machines. Mammoth tractors, digging furrows and dropping cane joints as seed, plant 15 acres or more a day. Planes spray insecticides and sometimes fertilizers. After 18 to 22 months the cane is ripe.

When harvesting starts, mills operate 24 hours a day for maximum efficiency. To keep the mills steadily supplied while making sure that a surplus does not accumulate and waste, harvesting schedules are set up, field by field. Following this schedule, fields are burned and then worked over by machines with huge claws. These snatch up the standing cane, leaving the roots for ratoons (second-growth crops from the same planting). The cane must be transported to the mills within 24 hours after harvesting, so that the juice will not have time to drip away or ferment in the stalks.

At the mill the cane is washed, the stalks are shredded, and the juice is squeezed out. The resulting liquid is boiled for twelve hours to produce raw sugar. Most of this is sent to the west coast for final processing and packaging in refineries owned by Hawaiian sugar companies.

Haleakala from across the bay at Maalaea

8,000 feet above the sea on the slopes of Haleakala, looking across the valley plain to the West Maui Mountains. On the right are the cities of Kahului and Wailuku (partly hidden by small cloud) and Molokai (in the background). On the left are Maalaea Bay and the tip of Lanai (at the left edge).

Petroglyphs at Olowalu, south of Lahaina

Cactus on the lower slopes of Haleakala

Haleakala Crater. High, clear, cold, and quiet. The silence is as unbelievable as the splendor. No words can match the photograph . . . and, beautiful as it is, the photograph is a pale memory of the experience.

If facts are useless, it might be a relief to turn to fancy, or at least legend. For it is perhaps only fitting that Haleakala is the one place visited by both of the two most popular legendary figures of Hawaii: the fire goddess, Pele, and the demi-god, Maui.

Before every eruption, Pele appears somewhere around the Island of Hawaii, often on lonely roads, in one of her two human forms: an old crone or a young women with red hair. Often she asks for some kind of assistance and woe unto those who refuse.

Trickster, prankster, scamp—Maui turns up in the legends of nearly all the Polynesian peoples. He is noted for his mischief, yet most of the stories about him involve generous acts of good will. Some say the story that he fished up the Hawaiian Islands belongs to New Zealand, but not Hawaii. Auwe! He raised the sky with his shoulders and flung it high, so that men could walk erect. One legend that certainly belongs to Hawaii is the story of how he snared the sun as it raced across the sky and forced it to slow down so that his mother would be able to dry her *kapa*. And, like Prometheus, he is given credit for bringing the gift of fire to men, this time in the form of the Hawaiian fire plow.

Curiously enough, several scholars maintain that the Island of Maui is not named after the demi-god.

A partial legend is the repeated statement that the *silversword* plant grows only in Haleakala, however examples have been reported on Hawaii; others may turn up in other places. It doesn't matter. By now the silversword is known as Haleakala's plant, and that is that.

It bursts into bloom only once during its life. Then it dies.

Wailua Falls (left), "two waters" tumbling hundreds of feet down the slopes of Haleakala, leaping to catch the light before they glide out to sea through Wailua Cove. Nearby you'll find *The Virgin by the Roadside* (below) sheltered in her black lava grotto. There is rarely an hour of the year, when this shrine is not graced by flowers left by a devout passerby.

The rugged rock promentories (top, right) are in the same general area. Closer to the town of Hana, some of these plateaus, covered with knee-high grass, are used for grazing cattle such as those on the slopes above the town (bottom, right).

Nearly smothered by foliage are *Hana Village* and the *Hana-Maui Hotel* (bottom, left). The cinder cone behind them is *Kauiki Head*. It was a lookout post and an invasion point in the struggles between Maui and Hawaii. It is best remembered, though, because a cave high on the ocean side was the birthplace of Kaahumanu, Kamehameha's favorite wife. Perhaps the fact that she was a Maui girl helps to account for her youthful beauty and lifelong high spirits.

Hana is often called "heavenly" although its enchantment is very much of this world and the good things in it. The use of the reverent adjective is understandable. Individual memories of Hana tend to blend into a single feeling of "this is how life *should* be"

The lasting memories of Hana are so often small, personal experiences that seemed quite ordinary at the time: the crisp chill of a mountain pool; the splashing of a waterfall muffled by cool foliage closing over the path behind you; the heavy scent of a sun-warmed plumeria tree in the late afternoon; the snug peace of a deserted cove; the lazy shade spread by the umbrellas of flamboyant trees over the road where you've stopped to gaze. None of these experiences is unique to Hana. It's just that Hana has the delightful gift of making the familiar seem fresh.

Whether it's the roads that won't let you speed, the gullied terrain that makes you watch where you're going, or some spirit of place, Hana tricks you into slowing down. It is almost as though a spirit throughout the area was offended at seeing you throw away so much of your life in mere haste.

After you've slowed down, Hana helps you recover the use of your senses. What had been mere impressions quicken into experiences. Although you've probably never been so relaxed, neither have you felt so alive. Perhaps it's right to call it "heavenly Hana"; there's something too real for this world about it. Although Maui's scenery can be pictured and its history can be told, the special lure of Maui remains elusive. Much of it must come from the spontaneous warmth and graceful pride of Maui's people.

Maui's attraction cannot be analyzed and is difficult to explain, yet it is strong and deep and it lasts.

MOLOKAI

the friendly island

Molokai is still largely a rural area, the home of
easy-going people whose old-fashioned courtesy has
earned the island's nickname. Much of Molokai's
escape from the confusion known as progress can be
explained by its geography.

The western half is a rolling plateau, perfect for
farming, but it has little water. The eastern half is
saturated with water held beneath steep mountain
slopes. The western half may be able to get water by:
tunneling through mountains to tap the eastern
reservoirs; converting sea water to fresh water; or
using brackish water for irrigation. Work has started
on all three methods, for Molokai soon may become a
giant truck farm for populous Oahu.

Meanwhile, there are more pure-blood Hawaiians
on Molokai than on any of the other islands, most of
them around the Hoolehua Homesteads area. This was
the first community started under Prince Jonah Kuhio's
Hawaiian Homes Act of 1921. It offered 99-year-leases
to those who were at least fifty-percent Hawaiian.

For too many years Molokai has been best-known
for the isolated settlement of Kalaupapa. Leprosy, now
known as Hansen's Disease, has been largely
controlled by modern science. Like the other residents
of Molokai, the gentle people of Kalaupapa are among
the friendliest persons you'll meet in the Islands.

Ranch on the south coast of east Molokai

Water lilies and, below them, Angel's Trumpets

Fish ponds along the south shore. These were used by ancient Hawaiians to store and fatten surplus fish and breed new fish.

St. Joseph's Church near Kamalo, built by Father Damien in 1876.

Hotel Molokai on the south shore of east Molokai

Charcoal maker on east Molokai, one of the last of its kind in use.
The lid is lowered on kiawe wood, which is cooked for about a week.

Roadside blooms

Fertility Rock, Palaau Park

Paperbark tree

The steep cliffs and deep valleys of Molokai's north shore.

"Old Hawaii" can still be found in isolated places. One of them is *Halawa Valley* (opposite) out on the eastern tip of Molokai.

Half a mile wide and three to four miles deep, Halawa Valley was once the home of hundreds of Hawaiians. Taro farmers and fishermen still lived here until the tidal wave of 1946. Today, fewer than a dozen people live in Halawa Valley.

On the way up the valley to Moaula Falls are terraces of taro patches, slowly disappearing under enveloping growth. Taro is a tuber whose root is used to make poi. Halawa Valley is a good place to gain an impression of how much skill and energy the Hawaiian had to use to get his staple food, poi, a very good food about which there have been too many bad jokes.

There are dry land taros, but the taro used for poi is planted under water, like rice. Considerable engineering skill was required, sometimes, to bring water to terraced, hillside patches and, always, to build the walls so that the patch would hold a large supply of water that was constantly moving, but moving slowly enough so that it wouldn't carry away any of the soil.

After eighteen months of growth the taro was harvested and the root baked in an *imu* (underground oven) for about four hours. This broke down small crystals in the root that irritated the mouth and digestive system. Then it was peeled, cut, and pounded with a large stone pestle. A little water was added gradually to form a paste. If it was to be stored for use later, little water was added, to slow down fermentation. If it was to be used soon, more water was added to give the paste a smoother, more fluid consistency.

It is an extremely nutritious food. A good source of vitamins A and B, poi is basically a starchy food. Unlike most starches, which tend to produce an acid reaction, poi produces an alkaline reaction in the body when it is digested. Before the war, visiting business-men discovered that poi was ideal for soothing and curing ulcers. Recently, doctors have found that many new-born babies who can't keep down cereal foods thrive on poi.

The Hawaiians called it *mai pake*, because it was known to be common in China. Entering the Islands sometime in the 1830's, leprosy made ruthless progress through the Hawaiian population. In 1865 the government started to try and curb its spread. Incurable cases were sent to the flat spade of land (above, right) at the base of the 2,000-3,000-foot-high cliffs barricading Molokai's north shore. The peninsula is *Makanalua*. Kalaupapa is the present settlement on the west coast, in the foreground. The original settlement, Kalawao, was on the east coast, behind *St. Philomena's Church* (left). There was a small clapboard church on this site to which Father Damien built the rock-and-plaster addition that forms the front two-thirds of the present church.

The first exiles arrived on January 6, 1866. For years boats called irregularly, dumping people and supplies overboard a few hundred yards off-shore, and leaving them to reach land as best they could with the ingoing tide.

Early arrivals found shelter in the few houses bought or built by the government. Later arrivals were forced out on to the open peninsula. From the lava rocks that litter the area, they built small, roofless shelters about five feet high. These always had their opening on the west side, away from the deflected trade winds that whine ceaselessly across the barren peninsula.

One result of these winds are the *rock bridges* (above, left), on the east coast. Wind-driven seas have hewn several of these arches, one inland of another. When the tide is low, and the sea is calm, these waters are good turtle-fishing grounds.

For less elegant eating, sweet potatoes were found to grow well in this unpromising land. They were used as a substitute for poi, when supplies were late, or failed to arrive at all. With inadequate funds from the legislature, the board of health did what it could to make life tolerable. They established a hospital, provided medicine for ordinary ailments, built a pipeline to bring fresh water from a nearby valley, and appointed a superintendent to bring some order to this community of the hopeless. Later, they moved the settlement to the healthier west coast of Kalaupapa.

In the early days, relatives or friends could come with the patient as *kokua* (helpers). Catholic and Protestant missionaries and laymen helped the patients for brief periods. In 1873, the Belgian priest, Father Damien, arrived and through his devotion and energy, soon made his presence felt. Although he discovered that he had the disease as early as 1876, he continued to work vigorously for, and with, his fellow-sufferers until his death on April 15, 1889.

During these bleak years on Molokai, a Norwegian scientist named Armauser Hansen discovered and isolated the bacterium of leprosy, which is now known as Hansen's Disease. Science now had an enemy that could be systematically studied and combatted, but the fight took years. In 1946 the discovery of sulphone drugs provided the means of arresting and controlling the disease. Today it's considered to be as contagious as tuberculosis, and takes about as long to curb.

There are about 200 residents of Kalaupapa today, many of them former patients. They prefer to stay there now that Kalaupapa has become in spirit, as well as fact, a part of the Friendly Island.

LANAI

the pineapple island

Lanai is pineapples, pineapples, pineapples, and no fooling. But to dismiss Lanai at this is to miss a good deal of interest.

Lanai is the only island whose name has passed into the English language without italics. Although it's now generally accepted as "porch", lanai originally meant a swelling, or hump, an accurate description of the island when it is seen from a distance.

Lanai was supposed to have been originally inhabited by ghosts. Then around the year 1000, the erring nephew of the king of Maui was banished to the island. He chased away the ghosts and made Lanai safe for humans.

With all the islands to choose from after his conquest, Kamehameha picked the southwest point of Lanai for a winter fishing resort.

Later, the ever-industrious Mormons turned its fields green with crops and spotted its hillsides with livestock. By the turn of the century, the land was being used solely to graze cattle.

Not notably successful for any other purpose, Lanai was ideal pineapple land. In 1922, the Hawaiian Pineapple Company bought almost the entire island for about $1,100,000.

The story of the pineapple industry gives a suggestion of how interdependent businesses are in Hawaii. Before they started, the pineapple growers studied and learned from the history of the sugar planters.

Once they had their crops harvested, however, they faced entirely new problems in distribution and marketing. The lessons learned by the pineapple industry are now being applied to Kona coffee, orchids, macadamia nuts, anthuriums, and, of all things, taro for poi.

Pineapples had been grown in Hawaii for a hundred years before they were developed as the Islands' second largest cash crop. The Spaniard Marin experimented with them while Kamehameha was still alive. Between 1880 and 1900 several groups began growing pineapple in commercial quantities on small plantations on Oahu and using primitive canning methods. Although he was not among the early developers, the story of pineapple in Hawaii centers around one man.

James D. Dole arrived in Hawaii in 1899. Dole believed that the future of pineapple lay in improving canning operations. He organized the Hawaiian Pineapple Company in 1901. In 1903 its first crop was canned into 1,893 cases. In 1906 the company built a cannery in the Iwilei district of Honolulu; today it is the largest fruit cannery in the world. The great development in pineapple canning came with the invention in 1913 of the Ginaca machine, which removes the shell and core of a pineapple in one swift operation.

On the agricultural side, pineapple growers learned from studying the achievements of sugar planters. After improving canning methods, the pineapple industry found itself up against a problem never faced by the sugar industry: marketing. They had thousands of cases of pineapple, but, outside the Islands, few people anywhere had the slightest idea of what a pineapple was or what it was for—or any interest in finding out. Dole started to create a market by advertising. One of his earliest ads read: "Pineapple—you eat it with a spoon, like a peach!" Following this lead, the growers, in 1908, then the packers, in 1912, formed associations that, among other activities, supported co-operative advertising campaigns. These made pineapples known and wanted throughout much of the world. In so doing, they also provided publicity that attracted interest to Hawaii.

In 1922, the Hawaiian Pineapple Company bought the island of Lanai (except for a few separately owned parcels of land) from the Baldwin family of Maui for $1,100,000. During the depression the company was absorbed by Castle and Cooke, where it was given Dole's name.

Today, more than 15,000 acres on Lanai are planted with pineapples, most of these on the western plateau from 1,500 to 2,000 feet above sea level. In the midst of these fields is Lanai City, whose 3,000 or so inhabitants have one business: growing and harvesting pineapples.

The pineapple is not a single fruit, but a cluster of small ones, each growing around an "eye" that develops from a pale blue flower. After plowing, the fields are covered with strips of machine-laid tarred mulch paper that controls moisture, raises soil temperature, and cuts down on weeds. Pineapples grow from shoots from an older plant. These still have to be planted by hand , about 17,000 shoots to an acre. The shoots are planted through holes in the mulch paper and take about 20 months to ripen into mature fruit.

One of the most attractive sights in the Islands, the neat pattern of pineapple fields was created for practical reasons. The direction of the planted rows helps control soil erosion. The fields are 130 feet wide so that they can be covered by the 65-foot boom on trucks travelling between the fields spraying insecticide, water or fertilizer. (Pineapple needs the iron sulphate mentioned earlier.)

During the summer harvesting season, pickers walk along the furrows between the rows of plants, snapping off the ripe fruit and tossing it on to a boom-held conveyor belt. This carries it to the truck that is carrying the boom. When a truck is full, it drives from under the boom and another truck immediately takes its place. All-day harvesting continues through the night, using floodlights on the boom. Workers wear heavy clothing, thick gloves, and goggles to protect them from the sharp spears of the leaves.

During the peak of the harvesting season, Lanai ships over a million "pines" a day by barge to Honolulu, where as many as six million pineapples a day are processed and canned in several forms.

Lanai does have forests, waterfalls, and deep gulches, but these are confined to the eastern slopes, and most of them are above the 2,000-foot elevation where maximum rainfall usually starts in Hawaii. (In general, maximum rainfall occurs between 2,000 to 6,000 feet above sea level.)

Lanai is a dry island for several reasons. It is a low, small island, lying too close to the lee shores of Molokai and Maui; the trade winds are forced to empty most of their clouds on these islands before they reach Lanai. Lanai is a low island; its highest point is 3,370 feet above sea level. The amount of land between this and the 2,000-foot level is small and receives an average rainfall of 42 inches. Lower areas on this windward, "rainy" side of Lanai average 12 inches of rain a year. (Areas considered to be nearly desert on Kauai have an average rainfall of between 10 and 20 inches.) Lanai is a small island of about 141 square miles; even if it lay directly in the path of the trades, its surface area could catch just so much rain. (Left side by side in the same downpour, a large, wide rain barrel will catch and hold more water than a small, narrow rainbarrel.)

Mountain reservoirs have been mentioned so often, that this might be a good place to explain what they are. Bearing in mind that this discussion is short and general and therefore can't be complete or cover exceptions, here's what happens and why it happens.

Most of the lava from Hawaii's mountains has cooled into basalt rock. Basalt is fairly porous. Even after a skin of soil has been formed to enable rain to run off in streams, much of the rain still sinks into and through the rocks until it reaches salt water that has seeped in from the ocean surrounding each island. The specific gravity of fresh water is less than that of salt water; not much less, but enough to save Hawaii's life. The fresh water "floats" on top of the salt water, the way cream used to float on top of milk in its bottle before homogenization. Because the fresh and salt waters are also in a container (the island mass), the steadily accumulating fresh water begins to rise a bit in the center. The increased weight then pushes down a bit in the center. Eventually you get what scientists call a fresh water "lens". This is an underground pool of fresh, pure water that is concave at the top a little bit above sea level. Whenever men tap this reservoir they try to get as far inland as possible, because the thin perimeter of the "lens" near the ocean is liable to have a noticeable percentage of salt water.

Lanai is pineapples, pineapples, pineapples . . . .

Kaumalapau Harbor

Unless history proves otherwise, these cliffs suggest that Kamehameha had an unexpectedly off-beat sense of humor. Whether they were being disciplined, or just proving their courage, some of Kamehameha's warriors were obliged to jump off the 60-foot cliff in the foreground into 12 feet of water. This was no great challenge to Hawaiians, except that they had to clear the 15-foot ledge of rock at the cliff's base. Those who failed didn't get a second chance. The cliff was named *"Kahekili's Jump"*. Kahekili was the tough, old Maui warrior (nicknamed the Thunderer) who for years was the chief obstacle to Kamehameha's ambition.

After his conquest was completed and he retired to Kailua, Kona, Kamehameha frequently came to this area on the southwest tip of Lanai for a vacation during the winter, possibly because of its excellent fishing. Although their residents have long since gone, the remains of 86 houses, 35 stone shelters, and other buildings of Kaunolu Village and nearby Halulu Heiau have been well preserved in the dry climate of Lanai. Here, too, are some of the petroglyphs showing the bird-like figures peculiar to Lanai.

Petroglyphs are designs or pictures scratched or carved on the surface of rocks. They can be produced by three main methods: bruising, rubbing a soft rock surface to produce a change of color; abrading, scraping the surface deeply with a hard rock; or pecking, hammering the surface with a hard, pointed rock that leaves a pitted surface. The designs are often patterns of simple forms: dots, arcs, or wavy lines. Pictures most often are of men; these range from simple stick figures to more sophisticated ones in which a recognizable muscular structure is suggested. Dogs are the next most frequent subject. Carving petroglyphs apparently died out among the Hawaiians about a hundred years ago. Although the stick figures are probably the earliest ones, nobody knows how far back they go, or when the first petroglyphs were carved in Hawaii.

Petroglyphs have been found on every major island in the group. The ones in the center picture, above, show a variation of the "birdman" figure that, so far, has been found only on Lanai. The petroglyphs shown on page 69 are painted; this is something that, apparently, was done only on Maui.

Who did them? Why were they done? What is their significance? These are questions that even the best-informed experts confess they are unable to answer.

You may surprise an antelope or a deer, but it'll be about the only sign of life in the *Garden of the Gods*. It is located off the northern tip of Lanai's central plateau, where the land begins to slope and gully its way to the sea. Here you'll find extreme examples of Lanai's dryness.

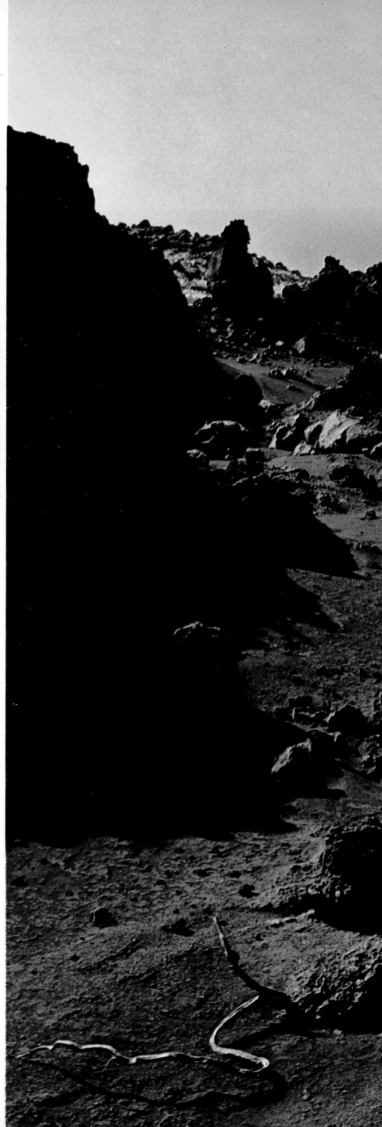

Lanai is a quiet place. So many have gone. The people who used to worship in the *deserted church at Keomuku* have long since left this little town on the road to Nahe, along the east coast. Today, Lanai's business is pineapples, not tourism. Yet for those who treasure quiet, and don't mind red dust, Lanai has its charms. Not the least of these is the kiawe-shaded seclusion of *Manele Beach* (above).

OAHU

the gathering place

Hawaii is a state of the union, a state of flux, and a state of mind. Nowhere else in the Islands is this more obvious than on the capital island of Oahu. All of Hawaii today is largely a result of what has happened on Oahu during the past two centuries.

The last two hundred years of this island's history start from the fact that Oahu has the port of Honolulu. Honolulu harbor was the only deep-sea port within a radius of two thousand miles. Fur traders and whalers discovered this. Merchants came to service the ships and stayed to use the land.

To work the land, they brought in people by the thousands. They built a new economy at a severe cost to an old civilization. The Reciprocity Treaty made sugar King in Hawaii and led to the overthrow of the Hawaiian Monarchy.

Almost as an afterthought, the Reciprocity Treaty also gave the United States the exclusive rights to the use of Pearl Harbor. The Navy didn't get around to exercising this right for thirty years. Today, the armed forces and other federal agencies are the largest sources of income for Hawaii.

Oahu's history is complex and its life rich in contrast. Yet on this bustling island there are still miles of beautiful beaches, many of them often deserted. There are shady valleys where you feel as though you're the only person in the world. There are parks where you can relax as though worry had never been invented.

Monarchs, missionaries, and merchants have all had their days on Oahu. Here you can have your days, too: warm, lazy days of quiet, and cool, soothing nights beside the moonlit sea.

Here's the story of Honolulu in one quick glance. A natural harbor beside the Pacific Ocean that attracted foreigners whose increasing numbers spread the city along the shores and up into the valleys and onto the mountains. Add Diamond Head in the background, beckoning visitors to Waikiki below it, and you have that touch that renders this story distinctively Hawaiian.

Not until 1786 did foreign ships begin visiting Hawaii regularly. These were traders taking furs from the northwest coast of North America to China. From about 1790 Hawaii began to acquire a resident foreign population.

Around 1794 ships discovered the reef-sheltered harbor of Honolulu, on Oahu, and began making it a regular port of call. Captains wanted fresh provisions and the crews wanted relaxation. Honolulu's development as a trading center began in 1795 and increased when Kamehameha moved to Waikiki in 1804. By 1810 Honolulu was becoming important commercially. With the only protected harbor within 2,000 miles, it attracted a growing number of ships.

Foreigners visiting Honolulu caused Hawaiians to congregate there. Honolulu, at this time, was a village of several hundred dwellings with as many as sixty white residents. Along the shore, traders stored their goods in thatched houses. Kamehameha did not allow foreigners to erect European-style dwellings or to own land. But, learning foreign ways, he began charging pilotage and wharfing fees.

In 1820, it was agreed that the new king, Liloliho, should settle in Honolulu, where he arrived in 1821. Up to 1820 furs divided the trade with sandalwood; after 1820 sandalwood dominated trade for a decade. Unlike his father, Kamehameha, the young king allowed the chiefs to share in the trade of sandalwood, an aromatic wood much in demand in China. The chiefs quickly went on a buying spree, buying everything on credit. To meet their debts, they took their people from their fishing and their farming and sent them to the cold, damp forests to cut sandalwood. The results were disastrous to the forests, the economy, and the people.

By 1823 there were four American mercantile houses in Honolulu. In 1820 an American agent for Commerce and Seamen had been appointed. In 1824 a British consul was appointed.

In addition to supplies, ocean-going ships need safe harborage, wharves, and rigging docks. Nature had given Honolulu the first; men supplied the second and third. By 1827 a shipyard was set up. But not until 1850 did the government begin dredging and filling to keep up with Honolulu's growth as a world port.

By 1829 the sandalwood trade was nearly at an end and the mercantile structure of Honolulu was shifting to a new base. Honolulu became a distributing center. Cargoes brought from the United States, Europe, and China were broken up, part being sold to the local market, and the rest combined into cargoes for re-shipment to other ports.

Local demand for foreign goods was increasing with the greater foreign population and the gradual westernizing of the Hawaiians' living habits. This growing local trade and increasing Pacific trade helped build up a substantial business community in the Islands, centered at Honolulu. Foreign trade shifted the population, bringing more people to the towns adjacent to ports and roadsteads.

Whalers began leaving their oil and whalebone in Honolulu and returning to the grounds for more hunting. The cargoes left were transshipped to New England on whalers going home, merchant ships destined to New England, or on fast clippers sent out especially for these cargoes.

This meant that whaling voyages were lengthened to as much as four years away from home port. Consequently, the whaling ships needed refitting and supplies, and Honolulu had facilities for supplying both. From the middle 1840's on, whalers bought more than half of Honolulu's imports and continued to buy a higher percentage each year. Whaling captains spent thousands of dollars a year for fresh provisions. A substantial part of the profits from the whaling industry went into the pockets of Honolulu businessmen.

The effects of this can be seen in the growth of Honolulu. In 1820 there was a population between three and four thousand, including fewer than a hundred foreigners. It was a village of grass houses, with half a dozen buildings of wood or stone. By 1840 the population had grown to about seven or eight thousand, including about 600 foreigners. By this time there were many substantial European-style buildings. There were well laid out streets and several two- and three-story buildings in the center of town. Honolulu was spreading toward Waikiki as far as the mission and beginning to climb up Nuuanu Valley.

Its growing importance brought the king and his court back from Lahaina. On August 31, 1850, Kamehameha III declared Honolulu to be a city and the capital of the kingdom.

The whaling fleets that had brought this prosperity were soon to disappear. Many people in Honolulu were beginning to be uneasy, feeling that rather than relying on the always uncertain whaling market, the kingdom's economy should be put on a more solid base. Attention was turned to developing the natural resources of the islands to produce a staple crop for export.

During the '50's the population of Honolulu, Lahaina, and Hilo was rising, but the population of the kingdom was declining. Every ship that had brought business to Hawaii had brought diseases, too. The effect on the handsome, robust Hawaiians was devastating. They had no resistance to foreign diseases.

The best estimates place the Hawaiian population between 250,000 and 300,000 at the time of Cook's arrival in 1778. By 1823 it had been slashed to 130,000. In 1853 the number was down to about 70,000; by 1866 it went down to 57,000; in 1872, less than 50,000. In 1890 there were about 40,000 Hawaiians in a land where a little over a hundred years before there had been more than a quarter of a million of them.

Disease kept the death rate high; absence helped keep the birth rate low. Hawaiians were excellent sailors. During the peak years of whaling, it has been estimated that one-fifth of the virile Hawaiian men in the prime of life were away from home.

Looking around for a replacement for whaling, the government came to agree with sugar planters that the economy might thrive on cane. Sugar cane needed, among other elements, a large supply of cheap labor. In 1850 the government passed the Masters and Servants Act, setting out conditions for the immigration and employment of contract labor.

In 1852, 293 Chinese were brought in to the kingdom as contract laborers. By the time the annexation resolution (1898) put a stop to their immigration, over 46,000 Chinese had come to Hawaii. In 1868 a group of 148 were the first Japanese to arrive. After the signing of a treaty with the Japanese government in 1886, they began to arrive in the thousands. By the time the "Gentlemen's Agreement" of 1907 all but ended their immigration, some 180,000 Japanese had come to Hawaii; about 126,000 left, some to go to the mainland, most to return to Japan.

In 1878 came the first Portuguese; 10,704 arrived before 1887. A later immigration from 1906 to 1913 brought 12,891 more. Most of them brought their wives and children, with the intention of settling here after their contract was over.

In the decade following annexation, about 5,000 Koreans arrived, as well as several thousand Puerto Ricans.

The Spanish-American War and the "Gentlemen's Agreement" resulted in the immigration of the last major group, the Filipinos. Starting in 1907, and increasing to large numbers in 1910, about 125,000 Filipinos have come to Hawaii. Of these, enough remained to form a substantial part of the population.

Before any of these people could be brought to the Islands to work, the planters had to have something to work: land, and plenty of it.

Compared to most of the other islands, Oahu has a high percentage of cultivable land. Yet, of the total area of all the islands, only about ten percent can be used for agriculture. No matter how it was used, in 1840, the king still owned all the land.

During the 1840's the Koloa Plantation on Kauai, though shaky, was demonstrating that sugar had commercial possibilities in Hawaii. Sugar plantations are an expensive investment and planters could not borrow money for the development of land they didn't own. Waterfront merchants were becoming nervous about having thousands of dollars tied up in stores and warehouses that could be whisked from under them. The missionaries were concerned about the worsening plight of the landless Hawaiian commoner who had no tangible stake in the new economy of his country. The king, himself, was deeply concerned about his people and began lengthy preliminaries towards working out a solution.

In 1848 Kamehameha III established the *Mahele*, or land division. This was an agreement between the king and the land-holding chiefs, in which each party relinquished any claim it might have to certain lands of the other in return for clear title to his own land.

The king then divided his own lands. Part were set aside as Crown Lands. These were the personal property of the king. Later, a court ruled that the lands belonged to the crown as an office, not a person. The king could use the lands and receive their revenues, but he must pass the lands on intact to his successor.

The other portion of his lands, the king voluntarily surrendered as government lands, to be used to help provide the expenses of running the government. By the summer of 1850, many of the chiefs had also given portions of their lands to the government.

In the summer of 1850 the legislature passed the Kuleana Grant of 1849. This was the central part of Kamehameha III's purpose in determining that "whoever had a share in making the land valuable had an interest in the land". Under this, commoners could make claim for ownership title to the lands they cultivated and to their houselots, providing these were not in Honolulu, Lahaina, or Hilo. The average size of a kuleana award was between two and three acres.

The Great Mahele and Kuleana Grant produced approximately these allotments: Crown Lands reserved for the king, 984,000 acres; lands granted to 245 chiefs, 1,619,000 acres; government lands, 1,495,000 acres; kuleana granted to 9,337 commoners, 28,000 acres.

In the original division, 1,000,000 acres had been set aside for granting to commoners; of this, only 28,000 acres were granted to only 9,337 commoners.

More than one critic has pointed to these figures as proof that the Hawaiian commoner was either swindled, naive, or lazy. Rather than argue, it might be of interest to consider one or two details.

To assign the entire 1,000,000 acres in three-acre grants would have required a population of one-third of a million, or about thirty-three or- four thousand more people than the highest estimate of the entire population when Cook arrived.

The population in 1853 was about 70,000. Three years earlier it might have been about, say, 75,000. Allowing a wife and three children per household (probably a modest number of children in those days) would leave 15,000 heads of households eligible to file claims. (This doesn't take into account bachelors and spinsters, but there's a limit to what can be done with a generality.) Actually, 13,514 claims were filed, but for various legal reasons the balance were not acceptable.

One of the two basic errors in this well-intentioned revolution was that the claimant had to come to the government to file, a process about which many of them had no knowledge. Had the government sent parties into the field to see who was actually on the land, explained his rights to him, and filed his claim or awarded his grant right there, probably there would have been a great many more claims awarded. The system was tried on a small scale in the Makawao District of Maui in 1846. Even though those claimants had to pay hard cash, once the process was explained to them nearly a hundred parcels were purchased in sizes from five to ten acres for a total of about nine hundred acres.

The other great lack was, of course, failing to make the ownership of the land inalienable. Even a twenty-five year period would have helped. As it was, too many Hawaiians did give away their land or sell it for a pittance.

One of the best known trade marks in the world, Diamond Head is seen here from its "other" side, with Waikiki above its slopes, Honolulu stretching beyond its peak, and the Waianae Mountains faintly visible in the distance. The Waianae, on the western side of the island, is the older of the two chains of mountains forming Oahu. The Koolau, along the eastern—or windward side—is younger. Eruptions from the Koolau filled the gap between the two chains, forming the central plateau around Wahiawa. Diamond Head, like Koko Head, is one of the later eruptions across the southern end of the Koolau.

Before condemning them as naive or irresponsible, it might be well to recall that Kamehameha the Conqueror had left behind him a still feudal kingdom with the old gods intact. He had been dead only thirty years when the Hawaiians were suddenly told to sink or swim with private property, a concept still strange to many of them. At the time of the Kuleana Grants, Hawaiians in their 70's had been children when Captain Cook came, stranger to them than a man from Mars would be to us.

The remarkable achievement of the Hawaiian is that he should have learned and mastered so much in so short a time and, though savagely reduced in numbers, managed to survive on his feet.

Then, on July 10, 1850, a law was passed giving aliens who resided in Hawaii the right to buy and hold land in fee simple, and to dispose of it to anyone living in Hawaii, whether Hawaiian subject or alien.

The door the Conqueror insisted on keeping firmly shut was now open wide.

Sugar needs the right climate, good soil, plenty of water, and, of course, people to plant, care for, and harvest it. Sugar also needs something Hawaii couldn't supply in large enough quantities: a market. This lay behind the tariff wall around the United States, a wall built solidly of 30% duty. This wall could be eliminated only by reciprocity or annexation. While they didn't like either, Hawaiian monarchs, understandably, preferred the first.

A reciprocity treaty meant that some, or all, of the goods of each country would be admitted duty-free into the other. Kamehameha III tried for one in 1848 and 1852. Kamehameha IV tried for one in 1855. Kamehameha V tried for one in 1867. (He delayed because it was considered "inconvenient and inexpedient" to talk business while America was preoccupied with the difficulties of the Civil War from 1861 to 1865). King Lunalilo tried for one, halfheartedly, in 1872. King Kalakaua tried for one in 1874 . . . and he got it! In 1876.

The treaty provided that unrefined sugar, rice, and most other Hawaiian products would be admitted duty free into the United States. In return, a long list of American products were to be admitted into Hawaii duty free. So long as the treaty remained in effect, Hawaii was not to sign a similar treaty with any other country. The treaty was for seven years. At any time after that, it could be terminated by either party after giving one year's notice of intention to do so.

Tucked in among all the international shopping lists of this treaty was the condition that Hawaii was not to lease or otherwise dispose of any of its ports, harbors, or other territory or grant any special privilege or rights to the use of them to any other power, state, or government. Not the sort of clause usually found in a trade agreement. But America had states along its west coast in an age when sailing ships were being replaced by steamships. These needed coaling stations and Hawaii is ideally located for any ship that proposes to operate on the Pacific Ocean.

The treaty was extended in 1884 and was being worked over for renewal when, in 1886, the Committee on Foreign Relations of the U.S. Senate inserted the exclusive rights to the harbor of Pearl River for use as a coaling and repair station. This clause threatened to kill the treaty. As it was, it toppled one government in Hawaii. Upon being reassured that the American government had no designs on its sovereignty, Hawaii renewed the treaty in 1887.

Although events leading up to it were suspenseful, the treaty itself was an anti-climax. The big boom started in 1876. The planters had a market. They could make money, borrow money to expand, and make even more money. The government suddenly found itself with more income than it knew what to do with, so it promptly found things to do with it. Kalakaua built a palace (today the only royal palace on American soil) and took a trip around the world, the first reigning king in history to do so.

Honolulu got itself all gussied up with wide paved roads, street lamps, telephones, streetcars, and an opera house.

Far from town, in the itchy dust of cane fields, laborers doggedly hacked out a new life for their healthy children. On hot plains on all the islands, planters sweated and cursed and got richer. In tall, cool rooms in Honolulu men became wealthy. And Hawaiians watched money growing on land where their grandparents had raised families.

Until the 1850's, anyone who wanted to travel to or from Hawaii by sea as a paid passenger had to make such arrangements as he could with the captains of the merchant vessels that made unscheduled stops at Honolulu. Then certain ships plying the Island-California run came to be regarded as fairly regular packets. In the '60's, transPacific steamship travel started between the West Coast and Australia and New Zealand.

Then regular steamship service was put on schedule between Honolulu and San Francisco, largely financed by government mail subsidies. In the '70's the new volume of bulk sugar required a whole fleet of ships for that purpose. Passenger volume increased noticeably and began to include visitors who were coming for pleasure, not business. A young Swedish captain was hired by Claus Spreckels for his sugar fleet. He did well and in 1901 organized his own steamship line. By the late 1920's William Matson's Navigation Company had a virtual monopoly on all Hawaii-mainland freight and passenger traffic and had built the Royal Hawaiian Hotel for passengers who had nowhere else to stay. Matson ships are still around, but so are other ships from all over the world.

Air travel to Hawaii started in San Francisco Bay and ended in Nawaliwili Harbor. Navy Commander John Rodgers and his crew of four in a flying boat were forced down at sea after $25\frac{1}{2}$ hours of flight. In 9 days they sailed 450 miles to the east coast of Kauai. But they had established a world's record by flying 1,870 miles over open sea.

Two years later, Army Lieutenants Maitland and Hegenberger made it successfully to Wheeler Field on Oahu in a Fokker Tri-motor. Two weeks later Ernest Smith and Emory Bronte, in a single-engined plane, made it safely to the top of a kiawe tree near Kamalo, Molokai.

In October, 1934, Kingsford-Smith and Taylor flew *from* Honolulu to Oakland, California, on the last leg of their flight from Australia.

Then Pan American added a dash of glamor to the dog days of the depression when, in 1936, their clippers started regular scheduled passenger service from San Francisco to Manila, via Honolulu.

The long distances of the Pacific War made Hawaii a center of air travel, foreshadowing its present role. Today the *control tower of Honolulu International Airport* (below) looks out over one of the busiest airports in the nation, where one plane discharges more passengers than arrived by ship during an entire month a hundred years ago.

The effects of the Reciprocity Treaty made annexation likely; the Spanish-American War made it inevitable. America had acquired Eastern Samoa in 1889 for its harbor of Pago Pago. Admiral Mahan had been chivvying the nation for years that America had a "manifest destiny" in the Pacific.

A coalition of shopkeepers and sugar planters had overthrown the Hawaiian Monarchy in 1892 and quickly offered their prize to the American Government.

President Cleveland turned them down in no uncertain terms. Rebuffed, the group set about assembling a government for their Republic of Hawaii. The interim Republic, like a doubting bride on the church steps, waited uneasily to be joined to another.

With American troops and ships in large numbers pausing in Hawaii on their way to the Philippines, the island government believed the time was ripe; this time the American government agreed. On August 12, 1898 the Polynesian islands of Hawaii became a part of the United States of America. Before the end of the month, American troops arrived on permanent assignment.

The first troops of a permanent garrison were an infantry regiment and a battalion of engineers, who set up a temporary camp on the land now occupied by the Honolulu Zoo. In 1907, the army began garrisoning its first permanent post, Fort Shafter, between the city and Pearl Harbor; this became army headquarters for the (by then) Territory.

Curiously enough, the Navy didn't do anything about its right to use Pearl Harbor, granted in the renewed treaty of 1887, until after annexation. Even then operations proceeded slowly over a period of about two decades.

After World War I had proved the value of aviation, the army air corps set up Luke Field on Ford Island in Pearl Harbor. They later turned this over to the navy after they had built Wheeler Field, up on the Wahiawa Plateau. It was next to Schofield Barracks, at one time the largest army post in the United States. This was followed by Hickam Field, now Hickam Air Force Base, between Pearl Harbor and Honolulu International Airport.

Today, the installations in Hawaii are headquarters for American military operations all over the Pacific, and the armed forces, with other federal expenditures, are Hawaii's largest single source of income.

There has been so much talk of bigness in some of these pages, that it is a relief, and perhaps of some interest, to point out that some of Hawaii's most interesting achievements today have nothing to do with size or money. They are, in large part, results of conditions unique to Hawaii.

Hawaii continues to fish, of course, not from outrigger canoes but from the *sampan fleets based at Kewalo Basin* (top, right), between the city and Waikiki. Out beyond Waikiki, around the Makapuu Point area, men are developing untapped ocean resources and studying how to build cities under the sea.

At the entrance to Manoa Valley, on the University of Hawaii campus, the East-West Center is creating a new and lasting understanding between community leaders and scholars from Asia and America.

From a museum built around a quiet old house on a hillside above Kaliki, scholars deploy over the Pacific, using the most modern scientific techniques to help discover and preserve the history and culture of the island peoples whose cousins pioneered Hawaii.

While jets whine overhead and motor traffic packs the shore-side highways, every ten days or so a big, white *Matson liner comes into Honolulu*. With greeting catamarans dancing around it (below, right), it eases past the *Aloha Tower* (left and right) to pier 8. The Royal Hawaiian Band plays island songs, boys dive for coins, Hawaiian girls dance a greeting, and the air is thick with streamers and happy shouts of greeting. For a brief, few moments the often chameleon-like present of bustling Oahu seems to change before your eyes to the easy days long past when Boat Day brought the gaiety and excitement of the whole city to the water's edge.

Here, in downtown Honolulu, are reminders of the last days of the Monarchy. *Iolani* ("Heavenly Bird") *Palace* (right, top) was started on King David Kalakaua's orders in 1879 and finished in 1882. On February 17, 1883 Kalakaua staged an elaborate coronation, witnessed by some 8,000 guests. So that they all could see the ceremonies, the actual crowning took place on a raised pavilion in front of the palace. Later this *pavilion* (top, left) was moved on to the palace lawn. Here the Royal Hawaiian Band plays concerts for office workers on their lunch hour. Two days after his coronation, King Kalakaua unveiled the idealized *statue of Kamehameha I* (bottom, right), across the street from the palace. This is the second casting of the statue. The first was lost at sea, later salvaged, and now stands near Kamehameha's birthplace in Kohala, on the Big Island.

The Monarchy has long since gone. Successive governments have come and gone after it. Hawaii had a Provisional Government in 1893, became a Republic in 1894, a Territory in 1900, and the 50th of the United States in 1959.

The cluster of grass houses around Honolulu Harbor has spread along the flat land out as far as Koko Head, up the mountain crests, and into the valleys. One of the newer of these semi-*suburbs* is (bottom, far left) above the Waialae Golf Course, with Black Point in the distance and Diamond Head off the picture to the right. Honolulu has even spread out to sea, at the *Ala Wai Boat Harbor* (bottom, near left), where about two hundred people live on boats the year round.

"I feel especially grateful that the discovery of our islands long ago was not couched in the context of an imperialistic and exploitive national power, but in the context of . . . the power of God," said The Reverend Abraham K. Akaka, pastor of Kawaiahao Church, in a sermon during a service giving thanks for the granting of statehood to Hawaii in 1959.

So much attention has been paid to the physical, political, and economic change in Hawaii, that there is the possibility of forgetting that many of the foreigners who came to Hawaii came to settle. With them they brought their families and their religious faiths.

117

The missionaries who arrived in 1820 were Congregationalists. The Catholics arrived first in 1827, but did not become firmly established until their re-entry in 1840. The first Mormons arrived in 1850, but they began their present growth after re-settlement at Laie in 1864.

The arrival of the first Chinese in 1852 began the establishment of Chinese temples, some Confucianist, some Taoist, some Buddhist.

In 1855, the Methodists started a church. In 1862, the Anglican (later Episcopal) Church arrived at the invitation of King Kamehameha IV and Queen Emma. The Lutherans were established in 1883 and the 7th Day Adventists in 1885.

Following the arrival of the first Japanese in 1885, five main forms of Mahayana Buddhism were established in Hawaii: Shingon, Jodo, Jodo Shin (Hongwanji), Zen (Soto), and Nichern. The Japanese also brought Shinto Shrines of many varieties.

The Salvation Army arrived in 1894, the Christian Scientists in 1902, the Northern Baptists in 1930, the Southern Baptists in 1940, the Unitarians in 1953, and the Presbyterians more recently. There are also meeting houses of the Religious Society of Friends (Quakers) and a Jewish Synagogue, established in 1950.

Much of the understanding between races that exists in Hawaii today can be traced to the fact that, whatever their personal feelings in a given situation, the people who came to Hawaii tried to live by a larger concept, a concept nurtured by their faiths.

They came from all over America, from all of the forty-eight states. From Alaska. From here, the Territory of Hawaii. Most of them went out across the battle-splattered Pacific to rank jungles, coral atolls, volcanic islands, to Korea, and Vietnam. They went forth to defend their country and lost their lives in that defense. Still in the middle of the ocean ironically named Pacific, they're back home now, in the fiftieth state of the America they died fighting for.

Near downtown Honolulu, is the crater of an extinct volcano. We call it Punchbowl; the Hawaiians called it *Puowaina:* "hill of sacrifice". Here is the National Memorial Cemetery of the Pacific, the final resting place of over 19,000 who lost their lives in World War II, Korea, and, now, Vietnam. Across 112 acres of soft, green grass dappled with shade trees, row after row after row of flat, grey stones mark their graves. On Memorial Day each grave is gently graced with a flower lei—a

leialoha, a "garland of love"—made by the schoolchildren of Oahu.

Those who didn't come back, who were never found, whose final resting place is "known only to God," are recorded in the eight Courts of the Missing flanking the wide steps of the Memorial. There are over 26,000 of them. At the top of the Memorial, above the Court of Honor, a thirty-foot figure holding a laurel branch watches over the young men remembered in the quiet of this hill of sacrifice.

Down the Memorial steps and along South Mall Drive, just beyond the third tree from the Memorial is grave number D 109: Ernest Taylor Pyle. Ernie Pyle is still in the company of the men with whom he slogged so many weary miles, whose danger and whose death he shared. Reporting the last landing he was to make, Ernie Pyle wrote what might be the epitaph for all those gallant young men resting forever in this *Puowaina:* "Our long ocean trip was over. Our time had run out. This was it."

Ala Moana Shopping Center may or may not be the largest in the world, but it's certainly the most cosmopolitan and probably the most fun to visit.

It's Disneyland with crackseed, haute couture in a muumuu, Saville Row in an aloha shirt. It has branches of Sears from the Mainland and a 300-year-old department store from Japan. It's a place where kids slither and clamber over free-form sculpture, and *pools of irridescent Japanese carp* (right) divide its malls. There are shops specializing in imports from Switzerland, India, the Philippines, Denmark, Thailand, Japan, Taiwan, and even Hawaii. You can dine in the world's first revolving restaurant, high atop the *Ala Moana Building* (above), or grab a snack from counters offering foods from Japan, Vienna, China, the American West, Korea, and corned beef in a kosher delicatessen owned by a Chinese-American. It's a place where security guards patrol parking lots in house-broken golf carts and a former beach boy has built a prosperous business in Hawaiian wear by advertising in pidgin English.

It's Oahu in miniature: the frantic energy (Hawaiian style), the shameless desire to make a buck (so long as the surf isn't up), and the carefree sense of fun where outdoor escalators carry the warning: CAUTION PERSONS WITH BAREFEET PLEASE USE STAIRWAY.

Right off the busiest part of Kalakaua Avenue (top, near right), in the heart of Waikiki, the *International Market Place* is about three acres of shops, eating places, and night clubs. It's more than that, though. It's a showplace, a meeting place, an open, shady, loafing place with inviting benches and tasty Pacific and American foods a lazy stroll away.

To open for business, many of the shops simply raise one of their bamboo walls; the friendly people running them are likely to be more interested in you than in selling you anything. Yet you *can* buy things here. Along with breezy Polynesian wear, you can buy sweaters from Hong Kong, handbags from Tonga, black coral jewelry from Maui, and crazy sweatshirts from who knows where. The mood is mainly Polynesian, though, with cuttings from which you can grow your own ti plant, liqueurs made only in Hawaii, and works by Polynesia's most famous modern painter. The "Artist Village" has some of the few authenticated *black velvets by Edgar Leeteg* (center, right) still available to the public.

The Market Place grew from a dream of the international restaurateur best known as Don the Beachcomber. Back in the fifties, when tall hotels began to replace tree-shaded homes, he worked to create a Polynesian grove where visitors could relax in informal surroundings. His "Tree for Two" is high in this banyan tree at the Market Place entrance where he has his own *private dining room* (above). His original Polynesian longhouse has now become Duke Kahanamoku's restaurant and night club, at the mountain side of the Market Place.

Across from it is the outdoor theater. Here the International Market Place Troupe presents free performances of the songs and dances of Hawaii, Tahiti, Tonga, Samoa, and Maori New Zealand, six nights of the week, every week of the year. Of the quarter-million or so people who see these shows each year, many have rated the International Market Place Troupe the best in Waikiki. On Sundays, they move onto the greensward, at the center of the Market Place, for a *noonday camera show* (bottom row, right). This includes the climbing of a coconut palm by a young Samoan and demonstrations of Polynesian arts and crafts.

Manoa Valley is the home of rainbows. It has riches beyond the conventional pot of gold for those who value truth and beauty. At the entrance to Manoa Valley is the University of Hawaii campus. Deep in the cool valley is Paradise Park, a lush treasure house of natural beauty, including these *parrots* and the varieties of *hibiscus*, the state flower.

Waikiki is a beach and place. Waikiki Beach, proper, used to be considered as solely that stretch of beach from in front of the Royal Hawaiian Hotel (the pink building) to the Moana Hotel (at the right edge of the picture). Nowadays it tends to include practically the whole stretch from the Hawaiian Village (in the distance) to the Queen's Surf.

Waikiki, the resort area, is bounded by the Ala Wai Canal on the Honolulu and mountain sides, Kapahulu Avenue on the Diamond Head side, and the ocean; some would include Kapiolani Park, lying between Kapahulu and Diamond Head.

After the capital settled in Honolulu, the *alii* and some of their friends began to build "country homes" in Waikiki. Kamehameha V had a summer cottage in a coconut grove on the site of the Royal Hawaiian Hotel. Although Waikiki is a hotbed of—among other things—tourism, tourism in Hawaii actually began downtown with the construction, in 1872, of the Hawaiian (later Royal Hawaiian) Hotel at the corner of Richards and Hotel Streets (the present site of the Armed Forces Y.M.C.A.).

Tourism moved out to Waikiki with the construction of the Moana Hotel in 1901. Tourism, and the Islands, received an unsettling boost with the arrival of Alexander Hume Ford. Surfing had all but died out and was practiced by only a few Hawaiians over in Lahaina. Ford discovered it, learned it, and with land from the Queen Emma estate established the Outrigger Canoe Club, in 1908, next to the Moana, and promoted surfing and Hawaii.

On the site of Helumoa, Kamehameha V's

summer cottage, the Seaside Hotel was built as a country annex of the downtown Royal Hawaiian Hotel. Beyond it a frame building and some adjacent bungalows were opened to the public as the Halekulani Hotel in 1917.

The Seaside was torn down in 1925 to make way for William Matson's fabulous pink palace of the Pacific, the Royal Hawaiian Hotel, opened in 1927, and still the queen of the beach.

In the same year, Mrs. Cassidy's boarding house (room and board for permanent guests: $60 a month) was replaced by the Niumalu Hotel down off Kalia Road. Before it disappeared in 1959, the Niumalu was the place where Anna Golbrait glazed her body with coconut oil and danced the solo Tahiti, the memory of which still causes some men to gaze into space with glazed eyes, and grow silent with awe. (Miss Golbrait later choreographed the Tahitian dances for the second filmed version of "Mutiny on the Bounty", but that, as Rudyard Kipling once commented, is another story.) The Niumalu was bought by the late Henry Kaiser in 1959 and on its site he built the Hawaiian Village, complete with a lagoon with its own coconut island. Hilton interests bought Kaiser's Village, added more profitable units (shown on the next page) and have since torn down the bungalows and two-story units and replaced them with condominiums.

One of the few marks of old Hawaii in Waikiki came to light when a bowling alley was torn down next to the Surf Rider Hotel. Four stones were revealed, the wizard stones, said to be invested with their powers by four ancient *kahuna* before they left to return to Tahiti sometime before Shakespeare was born. Part of these stones, on Kuhio Beach, are in the foreground of the picture at the lower right.

Luau is boiled taro (or Hawaiian *kalo*) leaves mixed with coconut milk; it looks like spinach, tastes something like sweet spinach, and is altogether delicious. It is also the name given to the feast at which it is served, because the proper name, *'aha'aina* ("great feast") probably was not commercial enough.

The feature dish at a luau is *Kalua pig* (top row, right). The name does not refer to the kind of pig, but rather to the way it is cooked ("*ka*-"the", *lua*-"pit"). The cleaned pig is rubbed inside with Hawaiian rock salt and, perhaps, some ginger, filled with hot volcanic rocks and tied together. Nearby, a fire has been burning in a pit lined with volcanic stones. The fire is swept out and the hot stones are covered with a thin layer of wet banana plant stalks. The pig is laid on this bed. Around it are placed more banana stalks and bundles of *laulau* (pieces of pork and fish surrounded by *luau* and wrapped in *ti* leaves). Banana leaves are laid over these. The pit is covered with canvas onto which earth is shoveled to seal it tight. The pig and its garnishes are left to steam for three or four hours. When uncovered and served at the luau the result is *ono* (delicious).

During a luau, whether commercial or country, there is bound to be a certain amount of dancing. (*Hula* is the Hawaiian word for dance). *Hula* in old Hawaii was primarily a religious practice with, as a result, a social purpose. Performers were carefully selected and trained. Judging by the few examples that have come down to us there probably was nothing very lascivious about these dances. The missionary objection to the *hula* was that it was a form of pagan religion, not that it was indecent—although they probably considered it to be that, too.

When the old religion was abandoned, the *hula* lost its main reason for being, but it never really died out. In 1833 Kamehameha III began a two-year revival of ancient sports and *hula*. Before becoming King, Kamehameha V encouraged the *hula*.

King Kalakaua is generally given credit for reviving the *hula*. As the above suggests, it wasn't really all that dead. Kalakaua did do two important things, though. He gathered together and set down as many of the old chants as he could find throughout the islands, before they were all lost completely. He also gathered many of the best *hula* instructors left and had them teach and build a troupe, which he subsidised and kept at court. For the first time since 1820, the *hula* had an official standing in the community and began being practiced more openly throughout the islands.

The *Kodak Hula Show* (both pages) began as a commercial promotion in 1937 and has since become an institution and one of the most popular attractions for visitors. On a plot of grass beside the sea just beyond the aquarium (in the trees in the background) there's an hour-and-a-half-long show designed especially for camera fans. It starts at 10 o'clock two to five mornings a week, depending on the time of year. Here are dancers wearing the Tahitian *otea* costume (bottom row), the Hawaiian *ti* leaf skirt (top and bottom rows, below) and the Hawaiian *holokuu* (center row), a fitted gown with a train.

Kapiolani Park is about 200 acres of land running from Kapahulu Avenue to the foot of Diamond Head and from Paki Avenue to the sea. It's Honolulu's big front yard—for picnics, play, and swimming.

It was opened by King Kalakaua on Kamehameha Day, June 11, 1877. For 25 years Kapiolani Park and Kamehameha Day were synonymous with horse racing in the islands. Then the races gave way to polo. Polo matches were held here on Sunday afternoons until a few years ago; now the area is used for rugby or soccer matches.

You can still feed the tame birds all over the park or visit the *Honolulu Zoo* (top, left) at the Waikiki end of the park. Down by the oceanside is the *Aquarium* (center, left), part of the University of Hawaii, where you can see most of the sea life found in island waters and watch seals and dolphins romping in an outdoor pool. Thousands have enjoyed entertainment under the stars at the *Waikiki Shell* (bottom, left), while hundreds enjoy the Sunday afternoon concerts by the Royal Hawaiian Band at the nearby brown rock bandstand, not shown in these pictures. Every Saturday the zoo fence along Monsarrat Avenue is the site of the *Art Mart* (bottom, right), showing works by forty island artists, some of them just beginning, some with international reputations. It's a sort of Montmartre in miniature, Hawaiian style.

Kapiolani Park also has tennis courts, picnic tables, golf and archery ranges, showers and rest room, lunch counters, the Queen's Surf restaurant and night club complex, a long stretch of beautiful beach, and sunsets like the one on the right. Some front yard!

Hawaii's international sport, surfing, was the sport
of kings in Hawaii before that name was applied to
racing. The *alii* of old Hawaii were big men, six
to seven feet tall, with the smooth muscles of a
swimmer and the trigger-quick reactions of natural
athletes. They needed them, for their boards were
big and heavy, too. Here we needn't rely on legend;
the Bishop Museum has some of their surf boards:
massive slabs of heavy koa wood, some as much as
16 feet long.

Today's boards are shorter and much lighter
(fibreglass-sealed, reinforced plastic foam weighing
about 25-35 pounds) but the surf can be just as high
as it was in the old days, and just as rough.

Oahu's north shore offers the most challenging
surf in the world during the months of January and
February, when the waves can come as high as
twenty or thirty feet at *Sunset Beach* (top left and
bottom far left). The International Surfing
Championships are held during December along
the west, or leeward, coast at *Makaha* (bottom,
near left). A more peaceful view of the same area is
shown (bottom, right) in the photo of Makaha
Beach Park, with the cone of Mauna Lahilahi in
the background.

In the middle of the pinefields around
Wahiawa, on the Leilehua Plateau, is a grove of
eucalyptus trees, sheltering *Kukaniloko, the
Hawaiian Birthstones* (top, right). At the end of two
rows of stones representing 36 high chiefs was the
important stone, Kukaniloko. To this came the
royal mother-to-be so that her child would be born
with honor. Established in the twelfth century, it
was, with Holoholoku on Kauai, one of the two
most sacred places for royal birth in the islands.

Falling 87 feet into a 50-foot-wide-gorge where it pauses to form a deep, cold pool, *Sacred Falls* (left) is on the windward coast, south of Hauula.

North of there is Laie, where, in 1864, Mormons, members of the Church of Jesus Christ of Latter-day Saints, purchased about 6,500 acres of land for a sugar plantation. Its profits supported the Mormon Church in Hawaii and missions throughout the Pacific. Gradually they developed the concept of making Laie the spiritual and educational centre of the Mormon Church in Polynesia.

In 1919, they built the *Mormon Temple* (top, right). In 1958, they built the Church College at Laie, the apex of a system that includes high schools in Independent and American Samoas, Tonga, Tahiti, and New Zealand. Then, in 1964, they opened the Polynesian Cultural Center.

Its 15 acres contain a lagoon and authentic reproductions of villages in Samoa, Maori New Zealand, Fiji, *Tahiti* (bottom, right), Hawaii, and Tonga. Part of the *Tongan Village* can be seen behind the bridge in the center photo. People in the villages are natives of the area represented; many of them are students at the Church College. They describe their respective cultures and demonstrate their crafts and arts.

After expenses have been taken care of, earnings from the center are used for scholarships to the Church College for qualifying high school graduates. Church college graduates return home, where their education, training, and experience help their entire community keep alive its own culture while dealing more effectively with the accelerating influences of Western civilization.

Makapuu Point, the southeastern tip of Oahu, is the pivot around which the pictures on these and the next few pages swing.

Almost on Makapuu Point itself is Sea Life Park (photos at left). Its serious business is oceanographic research, but it's a lot of fun for visitors. There are a Hawaiian fish pond, a reconstruction of the Hawaiian fishing village that once stood on the site, an ocean science theater, and, among many other features, the Leeward Isle Pool and Whaler's Cove. The latter has a 70-foot replica of the *whaling ship Essex* (below left), whose voyages inspired Melville's *Moby Dick*. Best-known and best-loved feature, though, are the porpoises. They frolic with the girls, play games among themselves, and even dance the hula.

Mokolii Island, better known as *Chinaman's Hat* (top, right), for obvious reasons, is at the north end of Kaneohe Bay. South of it, just above Makapuu Point, is the *Waimanalo* area (bottom, right). One afternoon in 1878, on her way home from visiting Maunawili, the Boyd ranch in this area, the lady who was to become Queen Liliuokalani composed *Aloha Oe*.

Koko Crater. Coast along its base shown in closer view, upper right.

Island artist sketching above Hanauma Bay

Blow Hole along Koko Crater shoreline

A view from the Pali Lookout
showing the coastal plain along Kaneohe Bay,
from Chinaman's Hat to Kailua.

If it hadn't been for Dr. William Hillebrand there might not be any Chinese or Portuguese people, or even mynah birds in the Islands. He was instrumental in introducing all three, as well as a good many tropical plants and trees, which he planted on his property. He came to Hawaii for his health in 1855. When he returned to his native Germany, several decades later, he sold his garden property to Captain and Mrs. Foster. When she died in 1930, Mrs. Foster bequeathed the by then good-sized tropical park to the city. *Foster Park Botanical Garden* (all of page at left) is just out of the down-town area, along the Pali highway. Its 20 acres of flowers and trees, rare and familiar, are all labeled.

The structure at the lower left is a Japanese shrine. In the center is the plumeria, or frangipani, or pua melia. Once scorned as a graveyard flower, in the last two or three decades it has become the most popular flower for leis. In the lower right are exotic forms introduced to the Islands, where they thrived beautifully.

Ula Mau Village (top, right), in Ala Moana Park, is a village where the arts and crafts of old Hawaii are practiced and its games are played. Everything here is as authentic as only acquired tradition and thorough research can make it. Started as part of the Aloha Week festivities after the war, the village (*Ulu Mau* means "ever growing") owes its present vitality to the dedicated energies of Herman and Malia Solomon and their staff of volunteers.

The *Bernice Pauahi Bishop Museum* (bottom, near right) was established in honor of the last princess of the Kamehameha line, by her husband, Charles Reed Bishop. The world center of research into the archeology, ethnology, and natural history of Polynesia; the museum is all that and a lot more. In its Kahili Room, just off the entrance hall, you can see some of the museum's literally priceless collection of feather cloaks and capes. There are displays that bring natural history to life.

Across the front lawn from the museum is its associated *Kilolani Planetarium* (bottom, far right), where, with the occasional accent on Pacific skies, astronomy is made as exciting as a spy movie and a great deal more interesting.

It was a sleepy Sunday morning. Many of the men from ships at Pearl were still ashore. The *Arizona* had an admiral on board. Some men were addressing Christmas cards. Some lay in their bunks eating tangerines, wedge by wedge. Some were grousing about the way their band had lost out in the "Battle of Music" last night.

On deck, the band began to get in formation for morning colors. A working party on the fantail was tying down a flapping awning as a windbreak for church services. It was a beautiful day. Even in December, by 7:53 in the morning, the sun was up and over Waikiki. In the sky the clouds were high and only a few dancing specks added a puzzling sight.

Then the specks became dive bombers, coming in four abreast down the channel, high level bombers from their rendezvous over Barber's Point, torpedo bombers glinting in the sun as they skimmed down from Wahiawa.

The alarm sounded. Below decks men still not awake responded automatically and headed for their stations on the double. One and then another shock sent them staggering against bulkheads and slipping down ladders. All they could hear was the shout of their own voices and the metallic chatter from the reverberation of whatever was going on above.

Somebody may have heard the first rending of metal. A few may have caught a glimpse of the searing flame before they felt it. Many may have been slammed by the concussion. Then,

nothing. In the wink of a few seconds, nearly a thousand men ceased to exist.

On the bridge, the admiral and the captain were dead. On the second deck, the entire ship's band was gone. Just disappeared. Its superstructure began to collapse like tired cardboard, and the *Arizona* sank into fifty feet of water.

At the end of the day, her oil-splattered colors, still flying defiantly, were lowered and taken away. Incredibly, 289 men survived. But 1,177 were killed, including 1002 for whom it will always be Sunday morning.

Today, a clean, chaste structure spans its hull; this is the *Arizona* Memorial. Or part of it. Much of it is below: the 1002 men still on board, still at their battle stations, forever on guard.

More of the *Arizona* Memorial is in the round-the-clock patrol of island waters by jet interceptors. It's in the search-and-rescue network spanning the Pacific. It's in the thousands of young men who've manned this fortress and then moved on west to protect it.

In a sense, perhaps all these islands are the *Arizona* Memorial. For half a century or more, whether they were driven by salvation or by sugar, men worked to get Hawaii into the United States. Then, suddenly, one Sunday morning the United States came to Hawaii as America's west coast moved 2,200 miles out into the Pacific, from which it cannot retreat.

These mountain tops are washed by waters that brought Polynesians from the south and foreigners from the east, and once brought enemies from the north. The waves that thunder against the black rocks of Hawaii beat against America's west coast. These islands in the midst of the endless, ceaseless ocean —and everyone on them—are the *Arizona* Memorial, and the steady thunder of waves is our warning.

This is Foster Gardens, near the heart of downtown Honolulu. Yet this picture could have been taken on any of the six islands we've visited. If beauty is in the eye of the beholder, perhaps enchantment is in the heart. All it needs is the stimulus to bring it alive, and the islands of Hawaii offer that in abundance. We have shared some of it with you, we wish we could share more. But for now all we can offer is Hawaii's greatest enchantment . . . ALOHA.

KAUAI

OAHU

MOLOKAI

■
HONOLULU

MAU

LANAI

HAWAII

■ *HILO*

Produced by Quest Travelbooks Ltd.
Book design by Geoffrey Traunter
Separations by Kal Opre:
Coast Colour Reproductions Ltd.
Copy consultant: G. John Norris
"USS Arizona" Official U.S. Navy Photo
"Death of Captain Cook" courtesy of
Maritime Museum, Victoria, B.C.
Leeteg velvet painting courtesy of
Lou Kreitzman, Artist Village, Waikiki
Typesetting by
Howarth & Smith Monotype Limited,
Toronto
Film: Ektachrome X (Eastman Kodak)
Camera: Hasselblad